Economics and the Environment: A Guide to the Economic Way of Thinking

David T. Geithman
New Jersey Institute of Technology

KENDALL/HUNT PUBLISHING COMPANY
4050 Westmark Drive   Dubuque, Iowa 52002

Cover photo by David T. Geithman.

For

Thelma,

Cynthia,

Kristina,

and

Jocelyn

Our planet is a lonely speck in the great enveloping cosmic dark. And in all this obscurity, in all the vastness, there is no hint that help will come from somewhere else to save us from ourselves. The only help is here. This distant image . . . tells me of our responsibility to deal more kindly with one another, and to preserve and cherish this pale blue dot, the only home our species have ever known.

Carl Sagan, astronomer, futurist and ecologist

The word 'feel' is used a lot in contemporary American education. I was surprised to hear my UCLA students' answers to economics questions with, 'I feel . . .' They seemed shocked when I cut them short and told them that economics is not about how you feel. It is about logical analysis and empirical evidence. This was clearly not what they were used to.

Thomas Sowell, economist

Economic theory teaches one how economic magnitudes are related, and how very complex and involved these relationships are . . . . No one can think about economic issues without some theory, for the facts and relationships are too involved to organize themselves: they do not simple fall into place. But if the theorist is untutored, he is apt to construct a very partial theory which blinds him to some of the possibilities.

I.M.D. Little, economist

Table of Contents

Foreword

American culture is forever in transformation. Those values held sacred by one generation are questioned by another. Jaded observers sit on the sidelines and comment how everything new seems old again. The history of environmentalism and environmental education is indicative of the ways that our culture grows and renews itself. In its first generation, environmentalism was rebellious, distrustful of corporations and the society that produced them. Today, such reactionism is no longer valid. Many environmental problems have been addressed and remediated since the birth of the contemporary environmental movement in the 1960s. Some commentators, like William K. Reilly, even go so far as to say: "The environment is the nation's foremost victory of modern social policy. The evidence is indisputable." Or, at least much evidence is indisputable: airborne lead emissions, sulfur dioxide, carbon monoxide, nitrogen dioxide — all have declined. Today, environmentalists and those in environmental education must realize that if society is to continue to protect the natural world, we must move beyond overstatement and oversimplification into greater rationality. This ecorealism, as Gregg Easterbrook has termed it, posits "that logic, not sentiment, is the best tool for safeguarding nature; that accurate understanding of the actual state of the environment will serve the Earth better than expressions of panic."

The book you are about to read is a study in rational thought. In the following pages, readers will learn the logic of applying economic analysis to environmental decision-making. Economic concepts such as opportunity cost, demand, supply, and marginal cost and benefit are, in reality, patterns of cognitive complexity, ways of thinking critically. As these rich concepts are applied to the state of the natural world, readers will gain an enhanced sense of the analytic foundations of environmentalism.

Will this mean that there is only truth and no beauty? Indeed not. There is a beauty in patterns of economic thinking, and it is appropriate that this elegance is applied to the protection and conservation of the natural world. In the analysis and extended case study that follows, David Geithman presents a framework for understanding the interrelationship of the human and the natural world. How much, he asks, are we willing to pay for pollution reduction? How may we achieve efficiency in environmental protection? These are tough questions, the kinds that some critics of environmental economics are apt to dismiss as positivistic or utilitarian. Nevertheless, in following the path led by economic thinking we come to understand that the best way to ensure a healthy and secure life for those who will follow us is to enhance our ability to think deeply.

Norbert Elliot
New Jersey Institute of Technology
Newark, New Jersey

Acknowledgments

Parts of this book first appeared, in much abbreviated form, as the economics component of a multidisciplinary book entitled *Environmental Protection: Solving Environmental Problems from Social Science and Humanities Perspectives* (Dubuque, Iowa: Kendall/Hunt Publishing Company, 1996). My co-authors for that book are also members of the faculty of the New Jersey Institute of Technology and recognized experts in their respective fields: Nancy Coppola (communications), Norbert Elliot (literature and rhetoric), Nancy L. Jackson (geography), Eric Katz (philosophy), and Burt Kimmelman (literature). To all of them go my gratitude and appreciation. Above all, I am indebted to Norbert Elliot for his continuing encouragement, advice, and friendship during the writing of both the earlier book as well as the present one.

I also wish to thank my brother, Theodore W. Geithman, and William Batkay for their help in the preparation of various drafts of this book, and the senior administration of the New Jersey Institute of Technology, whose support for the research and writing of this book over the past three years made the final result possible. Finally, any acknowledgment of my indebtedness would be incomplete without thanking my secretaries in the Department of Humanities and Social Sciences, Alfreda Anderson and Winifred Cummings, and especially my typist, Kelly Griffin, for her tireless and seemingly endless efforts in the preparation of the manuscript.

David T. Geithman
New Jersey Institute of Technology
Newark, New Jersey

Introduction

Every book has a purpose for being written and this one is no exception. The primary intent of this book is to introduce noneconomists to the special way in which mainstream economists view environmental problems and strategies. This "economic way of thinking" is often very different from widely shared cultural beliefs about environmentalism put forward by the media, specialists in other fields, and many environmental activists. The book is specifically designed with two groups of readers foremost in mind: First, the general audience of readers who are deeply concerned about environmental protection, who believe in the need for environmental regulation, but know little about how economists view these issues; and, second, college and university undergraduates, who are perhaps only beginning their studies of economics and environmentalism. The assumption is that neither audience is likely to have much, if any, previous training in economics.

Since the book is intended as an introduction to environmental economics for readers with little or no previous background in the field, all the basic economic concepts and principles necessary to follow the economic arguments — for example, opportunity cost, demand, supply, and marginal cost and benefit — are developed in the text as they are needed. The only prerequisite for reading and understanding the arguments of this book is an interest in learning how economics analyses the issues that surround the environmental debate at the beginning of the 21st century.

In presenting the "economic way of thinking" about environmental issues, two major themes emerge in the book. The first one is an extended critique of the command-and-control approach to environmental regulation, which dominates environmental protection and preservation efforts in the U. S. today. The alternative to the command-and-control approach, a market-based strategy of environmental regulation, is also examined. Because society must be centrally concerned with the cost of achieving its environmental goals and objectives, the relative economic efficiencies of a command-and-control approach versus a market-based approach to environmental regulation are of major importance to the future of environmentalism. Most people, environmentalists and nonenvironmentalists alike, tend to see the central questions as whether environmental regulation is necessary and, if so, how clean an environment do we want. For mainstream economists, the core issues are very different. From the economist's perspective, the central questions are how can society regulate the environment most effectively and efficiently and how clean an environment are we willing to pay for.

The second theme of this book — which is closely related to the first one — argues in favor of strengthening the rational, scientific orientation of environmentalism. Enhancing the analytical foundations of environmentalism will not be easy to achieve in view of the strong emotional and sentimental orientation of the American environmental movement. It is not uncommon for people to turn to emotional responses when they feel confused, displaced, or betrayed by the workings of the complex world around them, or to long for simple answers at a time when society is becoming more and more technical and mechanized every day. Moreover, analytical thinking and reasoning is much harder work than indulging emotions, fears, and superstitions. In his latest book, *The Road Less Traveled and Beyond*, M. Scott Peck, America's most widely read author on psychological and spiritual growth, emphasized how demanding rational thought is: "Thinking is difficult. Thinking is complex," he wrote. "And thinking is — more than anything else — a process, with a course or direction, a lapse of time, and a series of steps or stages that lead to some result." It is not through our reliance on reason that we go wrong, but through mental laziness, oversimplification, and stereotyping our reason is imperfect. "The remedy," he added, "is not the substitution of some other form of acquiring knowledge for rational apprehension; it is the education of our reason to be its true self."[1]

Redirecting environmentalism away from emotion and sentimentality toward greater reliance on rational analysis would allow the movement to be less dependent on the vagaries of subjectivism; to be more open to persuasion by empirical evidence; to be more respectful of the rights of others to hold differing views on environmental issues; and to be more accepting of compromise as a legitimate part of the democratic process. Changes like these would help the environmental movement to gain even more acceptance within the mainstream of American political life. Over the long-run, the American political mainstream has been dominated neither by statists, who would attempt to micromanage our lives to a degree inconsistent with traditional liberal Western values, nor by pure free marketeers, who would deny any social infringements on the rights of individuals even when they are necessary to achieve widely accepted social goals. The political mainstream recognizes the continuing need for an activist government, but also favors intervention that incorporates market-based mechanisms and incentives when they possess clear advantages over other forms of regulation. No other area of contemporary governmental regulation offers a stronger case, in terms of efficiency and cost, for the clear superiority of the market-based approach than does the area of environmental regulation.

Rational thinking does not necessarily mean having a fully comprehensive environmental policy that applies everywhere equally, addressing all environmental problems across the board. Nor does mainstream economics claim to have pat answers that embrace all past, present, and future environmental problems. But rational thought does require, at a minimum, having mechanisms in place for defining environmental problems consistently and for allowing a logical and coherent search for solutions.[2] By using economic thinking as a framework to help diagnose and analyze issues, this book hopes to provide a valuable model of systematic, logical thought that readers can rely on as they face the difficult task of developing their own integrated environmentalist perspective.

Outcomes of the Book

In this book you will develop an understanding of many of the concepts of economics, learn how to apply those concepts to environmental problems, and work through a case study concerning a socially optimal pollution abatement plan from the economic perspective. By the end of the book, you will be able to do the following:

- [ ] understand what the market mechanism is and how it works,
- [ ] understand the economist's concept of opportunity cost,
- [ ] define and identify negative externalities and relate these to market failure,
- [ ] learn how to correct for market failure,
- [ ] define and use the concepts of private benefit and cost, external benefit and cost, and social benefit and cost,
- [ ] apply these benefit and cost concepts to help identify and achieve an economically optimal amount of pollution abatement,
- [ ] learn to use a market-based system of incentives and tradable emissions permits as a means of achieving a socially optimal amount of pollution abatement at lowest possible cost.

Notes

1. M. Scott Peck, *The Road Less Traveled and Beyond: Spiritual Growth in an Age of Anxiety*, New York, Simon and Schuster, 1997, 25.
2. Daniel J. Fiorino, *Making Environmental Policy*, Berkeley, California, University of California Press, 1995, 225.

Chapter 1
Why Environmental Economics?

It would have been impossible thirty-five years ago to have imagined the social, economic, and political power wielded by today's environmentalist movement, to have anticipated the enactment of literally thousands of environmental laws and regulations at the municipal, county, state, and federal levels of government, or to have foreseen the extensive and largely sympathetic media coverage that accompanied it all. Today's environmentalism is, in great part, the legacy of Rachael Carson's Silent Spring, published in 1962. Designed to raise America's environmental consciousness, the book succeeded beyond anyone's expectations. A powerful indictment of past ecological abuses as well as a dramatic predication of impending ecological catastrophe, it helped turn a small naturalist and conservationist cause into a mass environmentalist movement firmly established in the mainstream of American culture.

One measure of environmentalism's growth was the expanding number of activist groups in the decade of the 1960s, like the African Wildlife Foundation (1961), the World Wildlife Fund (1961), the Environmental Defense Fund (1967), and the Council on Economic Priorities (1969). Over the same decade, the Wilderness Society went from 12,000 members to 54,000, while the Sierra Club membership grew by ten times between 1952 to 1969. But 1970 marked environmentalism's biggest growth year with the founding of the Center for Science in the Public Interest, Citizens for a Better Environment, Environmental Action, Friends of the Earth, the League of Conservation Voters, the Natural Resources Defense Council, and Save the Bay. The same year also marked the first Earth Day celebration. Greenpeace and Public Citizen were formed the following year.

The enshrinement of Carson's vision and the establishment of the environmentalist movement were grounded in the public's growing demands for governmental action to deal with a broad range of ecological problems, which collectively some were starting to call an "environmental crisis." Faced with popular pressures for environmental cleanup, protection, and preservation, whose physical dimensions and economic costs were just beginning to be glimpsed, governmental leaders acted. Almost without exception, they opted to rely upon a technology-based approach of top-to-bottom command-and-control environmental regulation rather than an indirect regulatory approach using market-based strategies and voluntary exchange, which are the primary means of conducting economic activities in the private sector.

Emotional Environmentalism

At the same time, the environmental movement became deeply rooted in a tradition of emotional argument and sentimental appeal, where Rachel Carson and her successors positioned environmentalism ever since *Silent Spring*. Doubtlessly, an environmentalism based on sentiment rather than reason meets many emotional needs. In the hands of skilled writers like Carson or Carl Sagan environmental sentimentalism can soar to inspirational heights (like the Sagan quotation at the beginning of this book). Others believe that environmentalism's emotional and sentimental approach is necessary to motivate large numbers of people in support of environmentalism and to forge the collective will to accept the huge economic costs and social dislocations that environmental cleanup and protection require. As one example, ecologists formerly implied that nature exists in a state of equilibrium and harmony, disrupted only by humans and their interventions into the environment. More recently, they have come to see nature as much more dynamic and changing, in a process of continuously becoming rather than as a fixed collection of life forms. This shift in perspective has spurred a debate among ecologists over whether the Endangered Species Act should be abandoned and replaced with more "holistic" legislation that focuses on preserving habitats and ecosystems rather than on saving individual species. The problem, however, as one biologist observed, is that ecosystems, "have no big, brown eyes to endear themselves to the public."[1] Similarly, according to Takacs, the term "biodiversity" was manufactured in the 1980s primarily to serve political ends. The word, he argues, conveys essentially the same meaning as "nature" or "wildlife" but with the addition of a scientific sheen, and is actually a political device intended as "a tool for a zealous defense of a particular social construction of nature."[2]

Like all pop culture based on sentiment, however, emotional environmentalism can offer only a set of overly simple answers supported by little serious analysis, an offering of strongly held opinion and ideology weakly supported by solid science. Emotional environmentalism fails to tell us as a society what our real choices are, but instead bombards us with frightening images of doom and gloom, tales of greed, exploitation, and depredation. Indeed, environmentalism has thrived, as Patricia Poore wrote in *Garbage* magazine, on emotionally loaded words like menace, catastrophic, collapse, shortage, disaster, breakdown, degradation, and deadly.[3]

The economic way of thinking provides a system of logical structure and analytical discipline, qualities that can help avoid some of the mental pitfalls in discussions about the environment. One such mental trap is thinking in emotionally powerful but uselessly simplistic terms. Helpful analysis of environmental issues is impossible as long as we are sidetracked by flamboyant, emotionally charged images like that of the valiant, but underfunded "good guys" versus the sinister, but politically and economically powerful "bad guys" doing battle for the future of the planet and the lives of yet unborn generations. Nor is environmentalism aided by sanctimonious portrayals of class struggle themes, such as suggested by the Executive Director of one conservation foundation: "It's no surprise that increasing unemployment leads to attacks on environmental controls by those favoring profits over health."[4] In the long-run, environmentalism cannot achieve its important goals by indulgence in such mental kitsch or crude stereotypes like the cartoon of a businessman who rubs his hands together gleefully as he oversees his smoke-belching factory and says something like "I never met a smokestack I didn't like." Tirades against "the polluters" only perpetuate the simplistic idea that pollution is the evil work of a small group of fat men with gold pocket watches and mammoth cigars who sit in banquet rooms all day on Wall Street. Self-congratulating images like these might make us *feel* better, knowing we count ourselves among the "good guys," but they have nothing to do with *reasoning* through the difficult issues surrounding the task of environmental protection.

Because of the enormous costs of environmental protection and cleanup it is crucial that society learn to regulate more effectively and efficiently. When it comes to the best methods for achieving environmental protection, economists often do not wear the same ideological glasses as many environmentalists. Those who look for "marks of Cain" in the people who run "bad corporations" and "big businesses" that pollute have learned little from the principles of economics. The idea that environmental degradation is caused by some awful character flaw or a gap in social consciousness perpetuates a myth that has made our current system of environmental protection far more bureaucratic, costly, and inefficient than necessary.

Notwithstanding the emotional mythmaking often present in our environmental literature, there has been a history of actual environmental abuses resulting in impaired human health and reduced lifespans; damaged buildings and other man-made structures; vegetation, forest, and water damage; reduced wildlife and even the extinction of some species; ruined recreational sites, polluted sunsets, and degraded natural vistas. Even so, public perceptions of environmental damages often are far more dramatic and pessimistic than actual threats, at least as far as hard evidence documents them. As serious as our past, present, and future environmental concerns are, an objective and dispassionate review of them hardly seems to correspond to such overdrawn descriptions as the following: "the worst crisis our country has ever faced" (Vice President Al Gore); "turning our world into a lifeless desert" (George Mitchell, majority leader of the U. S. Senate until 1994); "a greater threat to the Earth's lifesustaining systems than a nuclear war" (Gaylord Nelson, originator of Earth Day, former U.S. Senator, and now Wilderness Society lawyer); "the breakdown of society, and the irreversible disruption of the life support systems on this planet" (*A Blueprint for Survival*); or a "lemminglike march into environmental oblivion" (*Green Rage*).[5]

An Environmental Balance Sheet

A quarter-century of environmental regulation at the cost of more than a trillion dollars in environmental protection expense has created a far cleaner, safer nation than we might imagine. In many ways the environment is struggling back, although the successes never seem to make nearly the impression failures do. Looking back over the last 25 years, a balanced perspective includes both positive and negative experiences. The following list is merely suggestive:

☐ Of the 40 species of birds Rachel Carson predicted in *Silent Spring* would be wiped out because of massive use of pesticides, none have become extinct. For the 40 species, 19 have stable populations, 14 have increasing populations, and 7 are declining. Clearly, one of the major reasons for the failure of her prediction was the removal from the market of DDT, a non-biodegradable insecticide that built up in the environment and in living tissue, causing soft-shelled eggs in birds, thereby harming their reproductive capacity.

☐ Since Cleveland's Cuyahoga River caught fire and burned in 1969, roughly 60 percent of America's rivers, lakes, and coastlines have become fishable and swimable, which constitutes the Clean Water Act's specification of good water quality. In 1970, only about a quarter of U.S. rivers, lakes, and coastlines met the standard. The percentage of rivers failing tests for dissolved oxygen, phosphorus, dissolved cadmium, and dissolved lead has steadily declined since 1975, with only three percent of rivers now receiving the worst readings in these categories. Nevertheless, the 40 percent of U.S. waters that still fail the water quality standard received about 1.5 billion pounds of chemical discharges from 1990 to 1994. These discharges included heavy metals like arsenic and lead,which cause cancer or damage to the nervous and reproductive systems.

☐ As of 1992, all raw sewage generated in the U. S. is treated before discharge, usually in facilities that bring the residue to a standard safe for swimming. Ocean dumping of sludge also has ended in the U. S. Until the present decade, raw sludge was often dumped in even shallow ocean water offshore, where it sank to the bottom and could be easily taken up by the food chain.

☐ United States air quality is much better and healthier than it was in the early 1970s. According to regulatory standards, the number of days per year of "good" or "moderate" air quality in urban areas has risen steady since the 1970s, reaching 353 days/year in 1994. The total atmospheric emissions of lead declined by almost 60 percent from 1970 to 1980 (from 220 thousand tons to 75 thousand tons), and then from that level by another 93 percent from 1980 to 1994 (from 75 thousand tons to 5 thousand tons). The volume of particulate matter — tiny airborne particles spewed especially by trucks and older coal-fired power plants and industrial boilers — and sulfur dioxide emissions also declined dramatically. Nevertheless, the Environmental Protection Agency (EPA) estimates that 64,000 people (in the 239 surveyed urban areas) die prematurely each year of heart and lung ailments caused by particle air pollution.

☐ The U. S. greatly leads the rest of the world as the single greatest consumer of commercial energy — mainly oil and natural gas — with a total commercial energy consumption of 81,751 petajoules in 1993. (One petajoule is equivalent to about 950 trillion BTUs, or 163,400 United Nations standard barrels of oil.) This level is about ten times as high as the total commercial energy consumption level in all of Africa, eight times as high as in all of South America, and three-quarters as high as in all of Europe, including Russia.

Renewable sources of energy — windmills, solar panels, steam energy from deep in the earth — at present play almost no role in meeting U.S. energy needs. Even at its peak in 1987, renewable energy sources represented only four-tenths of a percent of total U.S. energy production, and by 1997 that share had fallen to two-tenths of a percent. The major reason for the failure of renewable energy sources to displace nonrenewable energy sources is that they cannot compete on a price basis with cheap power derived from fossil fuels. Many traditional utility companies have cut production costs and merged with other energy companies in the wake of deregulation and increased competition in the utilities industry, leading to lower power prices.

The U. S. relies far less on traditional energy sources than do many other countries. Traditional energy sources are forms of biomass, for the most part wood and animal dung. Traditional energy sources are renewable, but using them involves significant environmental hazards by way of striping extensive areas of land of vegetation and forest cover; removing potential fertilizer needed to replenish poor soils, in the case of dung; and massive, dangerous air pollution from burning both wood and dung. Total traditional energy consumption in the U. S. was 916 petajoules in 1993, compared with 4,815 petajoules in Africa, 2,748 petajoules in South America (— 2,021 petajoules in Brazil alone —), and 9,009 petajoules in Asia.

☐ The U. S. is the world's greatest single emitter of greenhouse gases. Greenhouse gases are those gases, occurring both naturally and through human activity, that enhance the capability of the earth's atmosphere to trap and retain heat energy. Many scientists, including the Intergovernmental Panel on Climate Change, believe that an increase in the atmospheric content of greenhouse gases due to human activities — primarily through burning of fossil fuels and forest clearings — has occurred, leading to the possibility of global warming. The most significant greenhouse gas caused by human activity is industrial carbon dioxide, of which the U. S. emitted 4,881,349 thousand metric tons in 1992, about one-fifth of the world's total. In that year, Africa emitted 715,773 thousand metric tons, Asia 7,118,317 thousand metric tons, and Europe 6,866,494 thousand metric tons.

Population Growth and Resource Depletion

To many environmentalists, the dual issues of world overpopulation and resource depletion are *the* central problems of the age. Notwithstanding real progress in dealing with pollution and other environmental concerns, they see the combined "crises" of population growth and resource depletion as threatening to "overwhelm the planet's carrying capacity," dooming the Earth to "complete ecological collapse." This view was a virtual article of faith at the United Nations' International Conference on Population and Development held in Cairo in 1994, and it remains a firm conviction for many environmental groups like the Worldwatch Institute, Zero Population Growth, and the Pew Global Stewardship Initiative. Yet such dire prophecies of ecological disaster, dating as far back as Parson Thomas Malthus (1766-1834), have never come true, at least not yet. Paul Ehrlich's *The Population Bomb* predicted in 1968, with "certainty ," that general crop failures would cause mass starvation in the U. S. by the 1980s, but instead the leading American agricultural problem of that decade was overproduction. Similarly, the Club of Rome report *The Limits to Growth*, written by Donella Meadows and others, predicted in 1972 an exhaustion of petroleum by the 1990s, but instead low international oil prices continue to reflect ample world petroleum supplies. Despite the profligate use of commercial energy by the U.S. and other developed economies, the planet does not seem to be close to running out of gas and oil in the near term. On the contrary, through a combination of increased exploration and improved extraction technologies, known world crude oil reserves actually *rose* by 50 percent between 1980 and 1990. Even more recent are the new oil reserves of the Falkland Islands, which could total 2.5 billion barrels — greater than the reserves of the North Sea. Although commercial drilling will not begin for at least five years, *The Times* of London has already labeled the Falklands "The New Kuwait."

Mass starvation due to population growth and resource depletion was almost universally predicted by environmentalists to occur in developing countries in the 1960s, 1970s, and 1980s, but, at least for now, life expectancies actually are increasing in the world's poor countries. The rate of growth of grain production in developing countries over the past thirty or so years has outstripped even their rapid rate of population growth. According to the International Food Policy Research Institute, from 1961 to 1994 population in these countries grew by 110 percent (from 2.1 billion to 4.4 billion people), but grain output grew by 178 percent, and grain production per person by 34 percent. Now, even their population growth rate seems to be subsiding. According to the latest figures from the United Nations Population Division covering 1990-1995, the annual population growth rate worldwide was 1.48 percent, significantly lower than the 1.57 percent annual rate projected by the previous United Nations report issued in 1994, just two years earlier. In the same 1990-1995 period, the fertility rate also declined to an average of 2.96 children per woman, from a previously projected figure of 3.1 children per woman. By the year 2050, United Nations analysts now estimate, the world's population could be 9.4 billion, nearly half a billion lower than the 1994 projections. Other data from a cross-sectional study of 98 low-income countries show a markedly *inverse* relationship between a country's total fertility rate and its real per capita income level: The higher a country's real Gross National Product, the lower its fertility rate.[6] Taken together, the data strongly imply that the process of economic growth itself can be relied upon to reduce a country's rate of population growth. The recent decline in the fertility rate reported by the United Nations Population Division seems to have its origin in rising living standards, as well as better education, more economic power and social status for women, and family planning programs that give couples more control over achieving the number of children they desire.[7]

Despite rising petroleum and grain production and declines in the rates of fertility and population growth, 9.4 million people on the planet in 2050 is a great many more than the present 5.8 billion, and each additional person is another mouth to feed and body to clothe. Conventional measures of a rising real per capita income relate to the production of goods, not directly to the resource base upon which all production ultimately depends. This resource base includes, but is not limited to, "natural capital" like soil and atmospheric structure, forests, fish populations, and petroleum and mineral deposits. (For more discussion of "natural capital," see Chapter Four.) Existing statistics on past growth of real income and agricultural production say nothing directly about impacts of growth on this resource base. They do not directly indicate to what extent past increases in income and agricultural production were realized by means of depleting the resource base.[8] On the other hand, if resources were being depleted, the normal expectation would be telltale rising prices of land, food, minerals, and energy. In general, these prices have not been rising, at least not consistently and across-the-board. Indeed, many resource prices have been declining for many years. (For a fuller discussion of the connection between population growth and resource prices, see the information box *An Economist and an Ecologist Make A Wager* in Chapter Three.) As usual, a balanced perspective is never a simple one. No other area of environmental concern reminds us more of F. Scott Fitzgerald's maxim: "The test of a first-rate intelligence is the ability to hold two opposed ideas in the mind at the same time and still retain the ability to function."

Love Canal

An interesting example of environmental exaggeration, even mythmaking — on a smaller scale, but no less illustrative of the power of emotion — is the story of Love Canal, a working class neighborhood in the suburbs of the city of Niagara Falls, New York. In the popular mind, Love Canal is remembered as the worst man-made environmental catastrophe in U.S. history, a symbol, in the words of one environmentalist, "for environmental pollutants of all kinds, the effluvia of an advanced industrial and technological machine." [9] Notwithstanding the conventional wisdom about Love Canal as "synonymous with the problem of hazardous chemical waste," in the words of then-U. S. Senator Al Gore,[10] it was largely a "disaster" that never really happened, at least in terms of actual threats to the health and safety of the Love Canal residents. For a fuller discussion of the incident, see the accompanying information box *Environmental History: Love Canal*. At bottom, the Love Canal episode appears to be primarily a story about dishonest scientific findings; a federal regulatory office, the Environmental Protection Agency, that pursued its own motives and agenda; irresponsible state and local politicians and health departments; and the image-creating power of the media in our high tech society.[11]

The Value of Economics

According to the economic way of thinking, society does not face the problem of choosing between preventing pollution or not preventing pollution. To the economist, such a choice represents the mental trap of either-or, black-and-white thinking. A more rational, although less emotion-

Environmental History: The Saga of Love Canal ———

In 1920 a partially dug and long-abandoned canal located in the Love Canal neighborhood of Niagara Falls, New York, was sold at public auction. For the next several decades the site was used by the city for garbage dumping, then by the U.S. Army, possibly for dumping chemical warfare material, and finally by Hooker Chemical Corp. for chemical waste dumping. By the standards of the time the dumping seemed not unreasonable, since the chemicals were buried in what was then considered to be impermeable clay through which there was no seepage.[1] In any event, the dumping ended in 1953, the property was covered over with dirt, and sold by its then-owner, Hooker Chemical, to the Niagara Falls Board of Education for $1. Hooker Chemical had originally resisted selling the vacant property to the School Board but eventually did sell under threats that the land would be seized under the doctrine of eminent domain to build a public school. Hooker Chemical had warned the city and the School Board about the dangers of penetrating or excavating the cap over the waste site, but soon after acquiring the land the city and School Board proceeded with the construction of storm sewers, roads, and utilities infrastructure.[2] Still later, home building began adjacent to the sixteen-acre rectangle that was once the dump, with the home buyers presumably being unaware that they were buying houses located next to a former dump site. An elementary school was opened near the corner of the now-forgotten canal to service the families that moved into the neighborhood.[3]

Resident complaints at Love Canal were soon being voiced, but they were largely ignored by local public health officials, the city government, and the New York State government. Neighborhood problems involved children being mysteriously burned while playing outdoors, foul and nauseous odors emanating from the ground, and multicolored sludge flooding residents' basements and surfacing in their backyards. By the early 1970s, buried waste had worked its way through the soil, into the water and the air of the neighborhood, creating "the archetypal homeowner's environmental horror story."[4] For a period of several years the residents received no satisfaction from their state and local health authorities or political officials. Besieged by a growing sense of danger and then near hysteria over both known and unknown health dangers, the Love Canal residents finally organized. Through a series of highly publicized appearances in 1977 and 1978 — involving the likes of then-U.S. Congressman Al Gore, TV personality Phil Donahue, and activist-actress Jane Fonda and her then-husband, politician Tom Hayden —

the Love Canal story received a steady drum-beat of intense, nationwide publicity. In several well-publicized confrontations with the New York State governor and other state and local politicians, the residents demanded action. An indication of the level of anger and fear that by now gripped the residents was the taking of several Environmental Protection Agency bureaucrats as hostages by Love Canal homeowners, who telephoned then-President Carter in Washington, D.C. to issue their demands for the hostages' release.[5] Ultimately, the problem had to be dealt with because it—and the accompanying media attention — would not simply go away. The government of New York and the federal government issued a series of emergency declarations and ordered three major Love Canal homeowner evacuations. In the end, 238 homes were purchased by the government and bulldozed, while many other homes farther away from the original canal were purchased and not destroyed.

These are all reasonably well-established facts surrounding the series of unfortunate events at Love Canal. But what were the actual health dangers to which the residents were subjected? Even now, those answers are far from clear. The EPA had conducted a study on chromosome breakage and other health hazards at Love Canal in 1979 and 1980. Their findings of an abnormal amount of chromosome breakage led President Carter to declare a health emergency at Love Canal in May 1980, only to have independent scientists subsequently review the EPA findings and reject them as flawed, tainted, unreliable, and unsystematic.[6] The residents themselves continued to insist that they were afflicted by a host of environmentally caused diseases and illnesses (among them, above normal numbers of miscarriages, birth defects, central nervous system problems, urinary track disorders, asthma, and other respiratory problems).[7] But when President Carter finally signed a bill evacuating families from Love Canal in October, 1980, the justification was not adverse pregnancies, chromosome damage, or dangerous chemical exposures, but mental anguish.[8] An official who spent the summer of 1981 working on epidemiological problems at Love Canal provided one expert opinion: "There is no demonstration of bona fide . . . health problems [at Love Canal]. As far as I am concerned, there is next to no good information [that has been gathered] in a bona fide fashion [that proves] people are adversely affected. . . . I have no question in my mind that there have been some pathologies at Love Canal, but I think it has all been psychological trauma."[9]

There is a final, ironic footnote to the unfortunate Love Canal story. In 1988 the federal government designated as habitable two-thirds of the homes that it had purchased at Love Canal but did not destroy. Young families, singles, and retirees eagerly bought them up. Although a row of still-deserted houses stands in a non-habitable zone, all the other homes have sold. According to the sales agent for the Area Revitalization Agency, the Love Canal neighborhood "is getting to be the place to live in Niagara Falls."[10]

Notes

1. Tom Tietenberg, *Environmental and Natural Resource Economics*, 4th ed., New York, Harper Collins, 1996, 457.

2. Dixie Lee Ray, *Environmental Overkill: Whatever Happened to Common Sense?*, New York, Harper Perennial, 1993, 138-9.

3. Lois Marie Gibbs, *Love Canal: My Story*, Albany, NY, State University Press of New York, 1982, 3.

4. Michael Silverstein, *The Environmental Factor*, Chicago, Ill.: Longman Financial Services Publishing, 1990, 72.

5. Gibb, 145-155.

6. Lee Clarke, *Acceptable Risk? Making Decisions in a Toxic Environment*, Berkeley, Calif.: University of California Press, 1989, 54.

7. Adeline Gordon Levine, *Love Canal: Science, Politics and People*, Lexington, Mass.: D.C. Heath, 1982.

8. Gibb, 5.

9. Interview with Philip Taylor, quoted in Clarke, 100.

10. Evelyn Nieves, "Love Canal: 'Houses Sell Themselves'," *New York Times*, July 21, 1996, 21.

ally friendly, viewpoint accepts that some amount of pollution and environmental degradation inescapably accompanies modern standards of living and populations levels, not to mention the impact of future economic and population growth.

Residuals and Recycling

Denying the inevitability of some environmental degradation verges on arguing with the laws of physics. The Law of Conservation of Matter and Energy guarantees that nothing simply disappears. The production and consumption of goods create residuals, and these residuals place pressure on the environment's ability to either dilute, chemically degrade, or simply accumulate them. All known technologies for processing or purifying these residuals in fact do not destroy them but only alter their form. Thus, discharging these residuals into one or another medium (air, water, land) or recycling them completely are the only available choices, and complete recycling is often very difficult, very costly, or altogether impossible from a practical technical viewpoint.

Plastic illustrates the physical problem in getting rid of our consumption residues. Much of plastic's bad reputation comes from the fact that it does not biodegrade,[12] but a new kind of biodegradable plastic has been developed. However, the new plastic does not end the disposal problem, and in fact may even represent a step backward. The commonly used definition of "biodegradable" plastic focuses on tensile strength, and plastics are said to "totally" degrade when their tensile strength is reduced by fifty percent. When that point occurs, which may require twenty years, a product made out of biodegradable plastic will have degenerated into many little plastic pieces, but the total volume of plastic will not have changed at all. The degeneration agent used in making biodegradable plastic, primarily cornstarch in most cases, comprises no more than six percent of the product's total volume; the remaining 94 percent of the product actually is physically more plastic than would be contained if the same product were made with non-biodegradable plastic, because products made with biodegradable plastic must be thicker to offset the weakening effect of the degenerating agent.[13]

When recycling is technically feasible, the recycling plants themselves often create unwanted by-products. One example is the newspaper recycling process, which must include the removal of the newspaper ink during recycling. One hundred tons of de-inked, or bleached fiber creates 40 tons of sludge, which then must be dumped, usually in a nearby landfill. Of course, all recycling efforts require the use of human labor, capital (buildings, plants, tools, equipment), and electricity. Recycling activities can be very labor intensive due to municipal curb-side pickups. As a result, the cost of labor and capital resources used can be many times more than the cost of the wood-fiber resources saved through recycling. The electricity required for recycling may use scarce *non-reproducible* energy resources (coal, petroleum) in order to save on *reproducible* natural resources (trees). Of course, the power generation that provides electricity to the recycling plants may itself cause air pollution. In summary , the net benefits to society from recycling are anything but straightforward. Recycling can result in saving some types of natural resources while increasing the usage of labor, capital and other natural resources. By no means is it clear that recycling always saves on total resources, and most likely it does not. When summing all the resources used in recycling, the *net* resources used by society for disposing of its unwanted by-products may be even greater with recycling than without it.

The Economist's Perspective

Because some amount of pollution or environmental degradation inescapably accompanies our modern world, environmental protection cannot be viewed as an either/or proposition. The realistic question is:

How much environmental protection does society wish to choose and pay for? Or, asking the question in a different way, How much pollution and environmental loss does society wish to accept? When environmental issues are presented as a choice between more or less, and at what cost, they become problems for economic analysis. Nevertheless, as economic theory began developing the central ideas of environmental economics during the 1960s and early 1970s, many environmentalists viewed with suspicion and even outright hostility *any role for economics* in environmental protection activities.[14] Environmentalists tended to see market forces as one of the primary causes of environmental problems and therefore they felt the need to override the market rather than to acknowledge its power. Policies were needed to oppose and reverse market forces, not to cooperate with them, they argued. It was, however, an irrational response, just as much as anger at the law of gravity is an irrational response when a paperweight slips out of your hand and crashes onto your foot. Even so, much of the U. S. environmental legislation embodies a clear antipathy toward market forces. The Clean Air Acts of 1970 and 1990 even forbid the use of cost-benefit analysis in helping determine air pollution abatement standards. The intent of the clean air legislation was to set air quality standards at a level that protects the environment and public health *without regard to cost*. (The legislation does allow for cost to be considered in selecting particular pollution control devices, but not in setting the standards themselves.)

Environmental economists, like other environmentalists, recognize the range of past, present, and future environmental abuses and threats. However, for the economist a realistic understanding of environmental issues also recognizes that environmental protection is often costly in the demands it makes on society's scarce resources. Consumption and investment activities other than environmental protection not only create their own demands on society's productive resources but, in the broader scheme of economic life, they make a far larger contribution to our real standard of living than does environmental protection. Untangling the tradeoffs between competing private and public environmental and nonenvironmental goals, analyzing the nature of their respective costs and benefits, and reconciling social needs with private needs are, for the economist, the focus of environmental analysis. In the interest of economic rationality, society must discover and compare the expected costs of environmental protection efforts with their expected benefits. Only then can it determine which environmental programs add more social benefit than cost and which add more cost than benefit to society. As we shall see in later chapters, comparing the costs and benefits of different environmental protection efforts leads to an analysis of an economically "optimal" amount of environmental protection that maximizes net social well-being. In almost all cases, the resulting amount of environmental protection implies *less than* complete environmental protection. The economically optimal amount of environmental protection very likely does not attempt to achieve a zero level of pollution.

Notes

1. John Horgan, "It's Not Easy Being Green," *New York Times Book Review*, January 12, 1997, 8.
2. David Takacs, *The Idea of Biodiversity: Philosophies of Paradise*, Baltimore, Johns Hopkins Press, 1996, as quoted by Horgan, 8.
3. Cited by Michael Sanera and Jane S. Shaw, "The ABCs of Environmental Myth," *Wall Street Journal*, Sept. 4, 1996, A-14.
4. David F. Moore, "Environmental Guards Must Remain," *Suburban Life of New Jersey*, June 22, 1994, 6.
5. The Gore, Mitchell, Nelson, *Blueprint for Survival*, and *Green Rage* quotations are all from Gregg Easterbrook, *A Moment on the Earth: The Coming Age of Environmental Optimism*, New York, Penguin Books, 1995, xiii-xiv.
6. Nancy Birdsall, *"Economic Approaches to Population Growth,"* in *Handbook of Development Economics*, Vol. 1, ed. by Hollis Chenery and T.N. Srinivasan, Amsterdam, North Holland Press, 1988, 477-542.
7. Barbara Crossette, "World Is Less Crowded Than Expected, the U.N. Reports," *New York Times*, International edition, November 17, 1996, 3. Also see M.J. Carvajal and David T. Geithman, *Family Planning and Family Size Determination*, Gainesville, FL., University Presses of Florida, 1976, and Theologos Homer Bonitsis and David T. Geithman, "Does Income Affect Fertility or Does Fertility Affect Income?," *Eastern Economic Journal*, 13,4, December, 1987, 447-451.
8. Pariah Dasgupta, "The Population Problem: Theory and Evidence," *Journal of Economic Literature*, 33, December 1995, 1883.
9. Murray Levine, "Introduction," in Lois Marie Gibbs, *Love Canal: My Story*, Albany, NY, State University Press of New York, 1982, xiii.
10. Al Gore, *Earth in the Balance*, New York, Houghton Mifflin, 1992, 4.
11. This is the judgement of Dr. Elizabeth Whelan in her definitive review of Love Canal, as cited by Dixie Lee Ray, *Environmental Overkill: Whatever Happened to Common Sense?*, New York, Harper Perenial, 1993, 140.
12. Society's attitude toward plastic has undergone a remarkable reversal. Far from the threat it suggests to many environmentalists today, in the early part of this century plastic appeared to offer the promise of ending mankind's dependence on natural materials like wood, steel, stone, rubber, and silk, all subject to scarcity and uncertain world supply networks. For these early visionaries, Jeffrey Meikle writes, plastic "would transfer the world from a crude, uncertain place into a stable environment of material abundance and startling artificial beauty." [*American Plastic: A Cultural History*. New Brunswick, NJ, Rutgers University Press, 1995, quoted by William Grimes, "From Bakelite to the Pink Flannel," *New York Times Book Review*, Jan. 14, 1996, 14.] To a remarkable degree, of course, plastic delivered on its promise, and our social criticism of the substance today is from the vantage point of a culture whose material standard of living is higher with

plastic than without it. The problems with plastic, as with petroleum, chemicals, and countless other products, stem from its misuse by consumers and producers, giving rise to negative consumption and production externalities. Negative externalities will be discussed in a later chapter.

13. William L. Rathje, "Rubbish," in *Facing the '90s - The Issues that Matter*, The Atlantic Monthly Co., 1993., 22-23. The article originally appeared in *The Atlantic Monthly*, December, 1989 issue.

14. Wallace E. Oates, "Introduction," *The Economics of the Environment*, ed. by Wallace E. Oates, Brookfield, VT, Edward Elgar, 1992, xiii.

Chapter 2
Command-and-Control
Regulation and Its Cost

The Nature of Command-and-Control Regulation

In the United States today command-and-control is the dominant form of environmental protection and regulation. The basic components of command-and-control are familiar precisely because they have been the mainstay of America's environmental protection efforts since the earliest beginning of environmental legislation. Command-and-control is best understood as an *approach* to environmentalism rather than as a system of environmental protection because it is not a coherent, integrated network of regulations. Instead, it offers a highly legalistic, top-to-bottom patchwork of overlapping, sometimes conflicting, and always controversial mandates, standards, and technology-based controls. The central features of this regulatory approach are sets of rules that either (1) mandate the use of specific pollution control devices on pollution sources, like double-walled underground storage tanks at neighborhood service stations, or smoke scrubbers on smokestacks to treat emissions of various industrial by-products; or (2) mandate strict emissions standards on amounts and types of pollutants that can be discharged into the air, water, or onto land by producers or consumers of specific products, such as the hydrocarbon, nitrogen dioxide, and carbon monoxide limits (in grams per mile) that are established for automobile exhaust emissions.

Some of the best-known Federal government environmental laws are the National Environmental Policy Act of 1970, the first modern environmental statute that required detailed environmental impact studies on federal projects; the Clear Air Act of 1970, which replaced a weak environmental statute with tough federal clean-air standards and timetables for industry to meet; the Federal Insecticide, Fungicide, and Rodenticide Act of 1972; the Safe Drinking Water Act of 1974; the Resource Conservation and Recovery Act of 1976, which established a permit system for disposal sites and regulated underground storage tanks; and the Comprehensive Environmental Response, Compensation, and Liability Act of 1980, better known as the "Superfund" Act. To this list can be added the Toxic Substances Control Act, the Asbestos Hazard Emergency Response Act, the Nuclear Waste Policy Act, and the Low-Level Waste Policy Act, plus dozens of other Federal acts regulating ocean dumping, pollution of inland nondrinking-water, and wildlife protection.

Most of the important environmental laws in America have been updated and amended one or more times since their original passage. Indeed, environmental legislation has proliferated to a degree rarely experienced in other regulatory areas. The U.S. operates under a federal form of government with fifty separate and sovereign states, each of which is concerned about pollution and environmental degradation. Consequently, the fifty individual states have created an additional fifty different sets of state environmental protection rules and regulations and fifty different state environmental protection agencies (under a variety of names) to enforce them. The agencies usually have the power to subject individual and business violators to fines, penalties, and, on occasion, jail sentences. As of 1993, Federal government regulations designed to screen out risky substances — only a tiny part of the country's overall environmental protection effort — were contained in at least twenty-six different Federal statutes administered by at least eight different Federal agencies,[1] the largest and best known of which is the Environmental Protection Agency (EPA). Agency rules and standards vary from program to program, sometimes denying permission to market a product, sometimes insisting on a cleanup, sometimes refusing permission to open a new plant or begin production of a new product.

Detailed environmental rules and standards are sometimes directly legislated by the U.S. Congress and the fifty state legislatures. Far more often, the actual regulatory rules and standards are written by the federal and state environmental agencies charged with enforcing them. Critics of this rulemaking authority describe it as unhealthy and "antidemocratic," because it can short-circuit public input or oversight on matters that often profoundly effect the lives of many people.[2] Others defend the process on the grounds that such rulemaking authority is delegated, either implicitly or explicity, to the regulatory agencies by the U.S. Congress and the various state legislatures. The limits and constraints on the practice of rulemaking by the regulatory agencies remain a vague and ambiguous area, and therefore the practice generates continuous controversy between the regulators and the regulated.

Blending Politics and Science

Controversial or not, it is nevertheless standard practice for state and federal regulatory agencies to routinely interpret U.S. Congressional and state legislative acts and elaborate them into specific rules, orders, mandates, and standards. However , the practice of delegating responsibility for environmental protection to the regulatory agencies goes beyond setting rules and standards. The agencies also are often responsible for the scientific review that later forms the basis for the standard-setting. An inherent conflict of interest may be created when a regulatory agency conducts research on the very environmental problems it regulates. "EPA," complained one scientist, "is doing EPA's research in EPA labs with EPA employees under EPA oversight. How could they not have a vested interest in the outcome?"[3] The problem is that regulators do not look at scientific data the same way scientists do. If various studies are performed on a particular environmental concern, say, the presence of dioxins in the environment, scientists usually follow the weight-of-evidence approach in evaluating the data. One or two positive findings are outweighed by 10 or 20 negative findings, all other things being equal. Not so in the regulatory arena, where one positive result may be enough to create a new rule or standard. "Regulatory agencies don't want to disprove anything; they just want to know if there is enough data to support a regulatory decision," complained one scientist-critic. "If the data are ambiguous, a regulatory agency will simply pick and choose the data that support its position and ignore the rest."[4]

The failure to keep environmental politics out of the scientific process was evident in a recent large-scale EPA study on dioxins, which took more than four years and several million dollars to produce. The EPA's position was that current dioxin levels pose unacceptable risks to human health, and therefore new and tougher standards on dioxin emissions from paper mills, incinerators, and other sources were necessary. To review its dioxin study the agency then selected an independent panel of 39 scientists, drawn largely from academia and chosen by the EPA for their expertise and objectivity. In a stunning indictment of the EPA's use of science in setting environmental policy, the scientific panel told the EPA that it could not agree with the study's characterization of dioxin risks to humans. The panel described the study's findings as not scientifically defensible, and that the EPA needed to go back to the drawing board and reconsider its conclusions.

Conflicts with Local Governments

Sometimes individual states and local governments enact standards and regulation that are more or less stringent than those established by the U.S. Congress, resulting in a collection of many different laws, rules, and codes across the country with little or no uniformity among them. Due to the patchwork nature of U.S. command-and-control environmental legislation, conflicts between Federal environmental agencies — notably the EPA — and state and local officials, lawmakers, and environmental agencies are common. In Virginia, for example, the EPA has been highly critical of state governmental officials for resisting a more vigorous enforcement of federal environmental laws. Virginia appealed to the U.S. Supreme Court the requirements of the 1990 amendments to the Clean Air Act that set-up a new system of air pollution permits that states are obligated to enforce. Virginia also blocked the EPA from adding several new sites to the federal list of most serious Superfund violations. Additionally, over the EPA's strong objections it enacted a law protecting companies from disclosure and punishment when the companies detect pollution violations in self-inspections and remedy them. In this and other areas of environmental regulation, Virginia contended that the EPA acted in a heavy-handed and rigid way, placing too much emphasis on prosecuting violations and collecting fines and not enough emphasis on less punitive actions, like negotiated consent orders.[5]

Other states, like Ohio and Pennsylvania, are also seen by the EPA as resisting and neglecting federal environmental laws.[6] By mid-1996, 18 separate states had passed laws similar to Virginia's that protect companies, who voluntarily identify and correct their own pollution violations, which the EPA views as too lenient on polluters.[7] In New York, too, the EPA concluded that air polluter fines were too few and too low, inspections too few, and the pursuit of polluters "minimal." According to the EPA, the ability of the New York environmental agency to seek out and punish polluters was greatly weakened in recent years, in part because of a decline in the number of state workers enforcing environmental laws. New York officials contended that the decline in the annual tally of pollution penalties did not necessarily mean the environment was suffering, but rather industries were complying more with environmental protection laws.[8]

The Costs of Command-and-Control Regulation

Command-and-control regulation is, by its very nature, highly inefficient. The micromanagement of millions of businesses, industries, and consumers creates an enormously costly and time-consuming flow of paperwork and legal expenses for both the regulatory agencies and the sectors they regulate, generating hundreds of thousands of lawsuits and providing a steady stream of income for many thousands of environmental lawyers and legal consultants. One concerned environmentalist estimates that the U. S. currently educates about ten times as many environmental lawyers as environmental engineers and scientists, and that our regulatory approach rewards them with salaries three times higher than their engineering and scientific counterparts. "The bureaucracy drives the paperwork," said one state commissioner of environmental protection, "and the paperwork ultimately drives the bureaucracy."[9]

This approach to environmental regulation has produced startling examples of the Law of Unintended Consequences.[10] The Superfund law, for example, requires that any firm generating, storing, or transporting hazardous wastes must pay to cleanup any wastes due to improper disposal. However, any firm that is the source of even one barrel of pollution dumped at a site can be held responsible for cleaning-up the entire site. When multiple parties are responsible for a cleanup at a Superfund site, a financially healthy company is often grouped with others whose financial viability is doubtful and made to pay more than its "fair share" even to the point of bankrupting the financially solid company. As a result, polluters, insurers, and the government become mired in court over who should pay for site cleanup. In some cases, *hundreds* of parties have gone to court over just one site. According to a study by the Institute for Civil Justice, during the late 1980s the EPA was spending more than seven times as many dollars on lawsuits, court costs, consultants' fees, and overhead than on actual site cleanups. By 1994 only about 50 sites were completely cleaned out of a list of 1,319 priority sites. As projected Superfund cleanup costs steadily escalate, independent evaluations of Superfund procedures and results have been very critical. A 1989 U.S. Congressional study, conducted by the Office of Technology Assessment, concluded that between one-half and three-quarters of all Superfund spending actually is "inefficient and undermines the environmental mission of the program."

Superfund administrators may be unintentionally discouraged from pursuing cost efficient cleanups. Because they have no incentive to concern themselves with cost they can, and often do, require very small increments of cleanup and risk reduction at very large additional cost to private businesses and individuals. The EPA may even have an incentive to inflate cleanup standards, and therefore cost, because the EPA's overhead charges inflate as well. These overhead charges are no small matter. According to a recently proposed Superfund rule change, for work performed on an earlier Superfund cleanup the EPA would be reimbursed between $269 and $376 of overhead for every hour of work performed by each of its employees on the cleanup. These overhead charges are above and beyond each worker's actual hourly wage and they apply whether the work was done by a senior engineer or a manual worker. Moreover, the same proposed Superfund rule change would prevent private parties from legally challenging the EPA's charges on grounds that such costs were unnecessary or unreasonable. In a case of the ultimate bureaucratic "Catch 22," there would be no restriction on what the EPA could spend and charge private parties and no legal way for these parties to defend against the charges, even if the EPA later admitted its standards were unnecessary and its bills unreasonable. Because of EPA standards and rules like these, large amounts of society's scarce resources are sometimes devoted to remedying relatively insignificant social risks.[11]

One of the first state industrial cleanup laws, the Environmental Cleanup Responsibility Act (ECRA), was adopted in 1983 in New Jersey by a legislature committed to reversing New Jersey's history of poor environmental responsibility. The law, which most environmentalists hailed at the time as great leap forward, required most commercial and industrial real estate in New Jersey to get a clean bill of environmental health before the property could be sold. Under ECRA, an entire site had to be cleaned before any building or part of the property could be leased or sold. The law's effect, however, unintentionally turned hundreds of older manufacturing sites, as well as other newer complexes, into abandoned and worthless "white elephants." According to the administrator of the ECRA program during its first five years, the law had a devastating impact on New Jersey's manufacturing sector and on the central cities in particular that housed many of its aging factories and plants.[12] Countless companies closed or moved out-of-state, with the resulting loss of thousands of jobs, millions of dollars in lost taxes, a shrunken local property tax base, and a negative "ripple effect" on dozens of local economies. "No other state in the nation," said the director of the Business and Commerce Association of New Jersey, "has to contend with a law like ECRA. That's why New Jersey manufacturing is on its way out."[13]

Because of the problems caused by ECRA, the New Jersey legislature adopted a reform bill in 1993 called the Industrial Site Recovery Act. According to its critics, however, the reform bill was also seriously flawed. For one thing, the new law failed to recognize the need for different standards of cleanup depending upon the eventual use of the property. Different cleanup standards can be necessary to promote redevelopment for tracts destined for industrial use, so called "brownfields." The "brownfield" tracts would not have to meet the same, higher standards as property destined for housing. Another problem with the new law was that it failed to reform the liability responsibility for cleanups. Like the federal Superfund legislation, state environmental laws are more inclined to penalize the parties with the "deepest pockets" rather than the worst polluters. An assembly operation, responsible for only 30 percent of the contaminated waste at a site, for example, could be compelled to pay 100 percent of the cleanup costs if it is financially capable of paying and the other polluters are not. Finally, the new law established *a one-in-a-million standard of lifetime risk* that had not been in ECRA. The lifetime risk standard in the new law implied that a property must be remediated to a safety level of just one additional cancer death per million population over a direct exposure period of 70 years to any potentially harmful substance. Implementing a one-in-a-million lifetime risk standard would likely cost *far more than* ten times as much as a one-in-a-100,000 risk standard.

The one-in-a-million standard of lifetime risk has been suggested for other areas of environmental protection besides industrial cleanup sites. EPA director Carol Browner has proposed banning any pesticide, for example, that poses a risk to food consumers in excess of one additional lifetime cancer death per million people. How does the standard of one-in-a-million lifetime risk compare with other risks from common human activities? Being hit and killed by lighting is 35 times greater that a one-in-a-million lifetime risk. Motor vehicles are 16,000 times riskier than the one-in-a-million lifetime risk standard. Applying the standard literally to ordinary activities would mean outlawing not only all automobiles, but also stairs, bicycles, airplanes, and golf courses. Nevertheless, the EPA proposal was presented without considering how the elimination of the effected pesticides would effect the cost of producing food. The best available estimates suggest that an EPA ban on all the effected pesticides under a one-in-a-million risk standard could raise the price of fruits and vegetables by as much as 50 percent.[14] There appears to be no reasonable balance between the likely cost of implementing the one-in-a-million standard and the expected life-saving benefit to be derived from the one-in-a-million standard.

The Burden of Regulatory Costs

Often the Superfund and other environmental protection programs are defended against charges of high costs and costs greatly in excess of expected benefits with the argument that, because of the "polluter pays" principle, ordinary Americans are not required to pay for Superfund cleanups and other forms of environmental protection. But, in reality, the average worker, taxpayer, and consumer does pay the bill, or most of it, not only for Superfund cleanup charges but other environmental protection costs as well.

Environmental protection and cleanup costs can be (a) open, aboveboard budgeted costs or (b) hidden costs, in which legislators and regulators spend public money without either a regulatory expenditure or tax appearing in a governmental budget. In the first category are the billions of dollars budgeted for Superfund cleanups. The original Superfund Act, passed in response to the Love Canal incident, included an initial $1.6 billion appropriation. In 1986 Congress added another $8.6 billion to the fund and another $5.1 billion in 1990 in response to perceptions of more and larger site cleanups, with the total Superfund cost seemingly destined to go very, very much higher. A U.S. government General Accounting Office study notes that the number of priority cleanup sites could grow to 4,000, with a price tag of $39 billion. A U.S. government Office of Technology Assessment study puts the potential numbers at 10,000 and $100 billion, respectively, while other unofficial estimates run upwards of a staggering $1 trillion covering 24,000 dump sites.

Other, more inclusive numbers show the budgeted cost of operating the 56 federal government agencies with various regulatory functions (including the Superfund and the EPA) topped $15.6 billion in fiscal 1995. The staff of the federal government's regulatory agencies in fiscal 1995 reached 132,690 bureaucrats, who were required to administer existing federal regulations and to write in 1995 alone an estimated 70,000 pages of new regulations (as published in the Federal Register), many of them involving air, water, land, garbage, chemical, and radioactive waste and pollution. The federal government budgeted costs, of course, do not include the additional billions of dollars of budgeted costs and thousands of additional bureaucrats working on environmental regulation at the state and local levels of government.

The second category of environmental protection costs are the hidden costs of regulation. These costs are both more complicated to understand and more difficult to measure. They account for the largest share of all environmental regulatory costs by a huge margin. Hidden costs fall into several categories: producer compliance costs, consumer compliance costs, and governmental compliance costs — almost all of which are paid by ordinary working persons and consumers. According to EPA estimates, private, nongovernmental compliance costs for consumers and producers amounted to $115 billion in 1990 alone. However, when compliance costs are estimated in terms of Gross Domestic Product (GDP) reduction, or what GDP would have been in the absence of clean air and water regulations, independent, non-EPA figures for the same year estimate that clean air and water regulations alone reduced the U. S. GDP by over $300 billion.[15]

Producer Compliance Costs

To producers, a cost designated as either a Superfund cleanup charge or any other environmental protection charge is just another operating cost, like wages and salaries, raw materials, taxes, interest, etc. Like all other operating costs, they must be passed along to customers in the form of higher selling prices for goods produced and sold, or to insurance companies, which in turn raise premiums to their customers. When producers cannot pass along these environmental charges — largely due to limits placed on them from the competition of other firms in the market — the effects will be similar to the general situation when a producer cannot recover other costs of production in its final selling price. Other things being equal, when producers cannot pass along their costs in the prices of goods sold, they either curtail production or go out of business. Consequently, fewer jobs will be generated, a notable result of New Jersey's ECRA legislation. The destruction of jobs of working people is a classic way in which ordinary people bear the hidden cost of environmental cleanup and protection. In addition to reducing the number of jobs, regulatory costs also may play a contributory role in the wage stagnation that has plagued the U.S. in recent years. Another hidden cost of environmental protection charges that cause firms to curtail production or go out of business can be a reduction in the amount and selection of goods available to consumers.

Consumer Compliance Costs

An example of a compliance cost borne by consumers is the cost of the safety and emissions equipment now mandated for all U.S. automobiles. According to the U.S. Bureau of Labor Statistics, environmental and safety regulations account for about 17 percent ($3,000) of today's average $18,500 automobile price. Assuming a total of 15 million new car and truck units bought each year, the current consumer safety and emissions compliance cost amounts to $48 billion per year. One result is that new cars are getting steadily harder for average families to afford, especially for families headed by younger people. A few statistics from the Census Bureau and the U.S. Commerce Department, together with new car prices, demonstrate the scale of the problem: When children born in the 1940s were aged 25 to 34 in 1974, they needed to work an average of only 21.7 weeks to pay for a typical new car. When children born in the 1950s were aged 25 to 34 in 1984, they needed to work 31.9 weeks to buy a car, almost 50 percent more in wage-adjusted real cost. And when children born in the 1960s were the same age in 1994, they needed 36.2 weeks to purchase a car, another 14 percent increase in wage-adjusted real cost.[16]

As we have seen in Chapter One, America's environmental protection expenditures have purchased dramatic improvements in U.S. air quality since 1970, when the original Clean Air Act was passed. In fact, the air is 90 percent cleaner today than it was in the 1960s as automakers have cut tailpipe emissions by 96 percent since 1970. Nevertheless, the 1990 Clean Air Act (amending the original 1970 act) requires auto makers to cut the remaining tailpipe emissions in half, bringing the emissions reductions to 98 percent. It also mandates the installation of devices to catch gasoline fumes during refueling and the reduction of toxic pollution at automobile assembly plants. By the year 2000, according to the American Automobile Association, consumers' emissions compliance costs could rise by an additional $2,000 per car, or an additional $30 billion per year, as more and tougher rules are phased-in. Additional automobile prices hikes of unknown size will be passed-on to consumers due to the costs of developing electric cars, which are now mandated for California by 1998 and under consideration by twelve other states in the Northeast.

Most of these new regulatory requirements have been established without solid scientific and economic support. Few estimates exist of the actual harm caused by the remaining air pollution the tougher tailpipe emissions standards are designed to prevent, and even fewer estimates exist of what it will cost consumers to reduce emissions by another 50 percent. As the President of the American Automobile Association noted, the EPA seems to ignore asking how much air quality benefit consumers will receive for the dollars they will spend. Other critics argue that, in view of the huge air-quality improvements that have already been achieved, it is unwise to use valuable economic resources to go any further. Nevertheless, in mid-1994 the EPA ruled that an expensive fuel additive, ethanol, must be used in 30 percent of all reformulated gasoline in many states as an additional means of lowering air pollution caused by automobiles. According to then-U.S. Senator Bill Bradley, the ethanol fuel requirement alone adds many hundreds of millions of dollars to consumer driving costs each year, even though not a single major environmental organization has come forward to defend ethanol. The Sierra Club and the North Eastern Air Quality Managers testified against the mandate before the U.S. Congress, and even the EPA admitted that ethanol's effect on air quality is negligible.

Government Compliance Costs

Government, too, experiences costs of complying with environmental regulations, which, of course, are passed along to ordinary Americans in the form of higher taxes and in less visible ways. As we have seen, when producers cannot pass along their regulatory costs in higher selling prices, they may curtail or close down operations. When this occurs, not only are jobs destroyed but the local property tax base shrinks; other things being equal, a smaller property tax base creates higher property taxes for all other business and residential real estate.

But government compliance costs are not limited to higher property taxes caused by a shrunken local property tax base. A decade ago, the "garbage barge" became a vivid symbol of environmental crisis. As Americans produced more and more trash, some landfills were thought to be reaching their capacity, while others were being closed for environmental reasons. To avoid fears of their own "garbage barge" problems, local governments everywhere spent billions of dollars building new dumps and waste incinerators, while the private sector, seeing the need for more waste handling capacity, also developed new landfills of its own. Now, local governments like Montgomery County in Maryland, Fairfax County in Virginia, and Dade County in Florida find they do not have *enough trash* to pay the debt they incurred to build the facilities. With all the public and private competition for the available trash and garbage supply, tipping fees — the money trash handlers pay to dump — have fallen, reducing local governments' revenues. Competition has become so intense that some local governments have had to raise property taxes to compensate for their lost tipping revenue.[17]

An interesting example of waste hauling and its consequences for local government compliance costs comes from New Jersey. Almost all the county governments in New Jersey were induced by the state to construct expensive waste disposal facilities, which added to total county indebtedness by nearly $2 billion. The county governments built the incinerators because, under command-and-control state regulations that directed all trash haulers in the state where to dump their waste, the counties were assured of a captive stream of trash. One result of the state's system of waste flow orders was that garbage disposal costs for the municipalities, and thus for local taxpayers, averaged about $75 per ton, well above the typical $30 to $50 per ton cost at other dumps in the Northeast and among the highest tipping fees in the entire country.[18] Because of the excess capacity of some of these county waste incinerators, the incinerators actively bid in the spot market to *import* waste from out-of-state to burn in-state. Their very large capacities and the competition for waste from other incinerators mean that some New Jersey county incinerators charge such low prices for out-of-state waste they are actually subsidizing out-of-state waste disposal.[19]

An ironic twist was given to New Jersey's waste disposal operations when a recent federal court ruling struck down the state's system of waste-flow orders that directed waste haulers where to dump their trash. The waste-flow orders were deemed unconstitutional because they interfered with interstate commerce, and they will soon be replaced by an open market system. County incinerators, which often have charged captive waste haulers twice as much as out-of-state landfills, will be forced to compete with lower tipping fees or lose their customers once haulers are no longer required to send their garbage to specific sites in-state. Tipping fees charged to municipalities are likely to fall by an estimated 30 to 40 percent due to competition for garbage. It is also likely that some or all of the burden of paying off the nearly $2 billion of indebtedness incurred by the counties to construct the incinerators will revert to the municipalities. The municipalities, in turn, will pass the debt cost on to local property owners in the form of higher property taxes. Whether it is paid at the state, county, or municipal level, a tax levy sufficient to pay off the incinerator indebtedness would amount to about $450 for every taxpayer in the state.[20]

Command-and-Control Regulation: An Overview

The main message to come from this brief review of America's environmental regulatory strategy and its cost is one of institutionalized inefficiency. U.S. environmental regulation is still primarily of the command-and-control variety, an approach that attempts to micromanage millions of producers and consumers while over-specifying compliance strategies and preventing innovation from reducing compliance costs. Most of the program-specific, cost-benefit research that has been done by economists shows that the pattern of American environmental protection spending is ill-conceived, poorly focused, and fails to accomplish the most good for the least cost. As we shall see in subsequent chapters, too little attention is paid to some environmental risks, while too much is spent on other environmental risks.[21]

Notes

1. Stephen Breyer, *Breaking the Vicious Circle: Toward Effective Risk Regulation*, Cambridge, Mass, Harvard University Press, 1993, 8.

2. Eric Peters, "Legislation Without Representation," *Wall Street Journal*, November 15, 1996, 14.

3. Quoted in Kathryn E. Kelly, "Cleaning Up EPA's Dioxin Mess," *Wall Street Journal*, June 29, 1995, A-16.

4. Quoted in Kelly, A-16.

5. John H. Cushman Jr., "Virginia Seen as Undercutting U.S. Environmental Rules," *New York Times*, January 19, 1997, 22.

6. John H. Cushman Jr., "States Neglecting Pollution Rules, White House Says," *New York Times*, December 15, 1996, 1.

7. John H. Cushman Jr., "Many States Give Polluting Firms New Protections," *New York Times*, April 7, 1996, 1.

8. Andrew C. Revkin, "Pataki Bolsters State's Pursuit of Air Polluters," *New York Times*, February 1, 1997, 1.

9. Gordon Bishop, "DEP Urged to Reject 'Political' Agendas," Newark Star Ledger, September 28, 1994, 18.

10. As Irving Kristol defined the idea, the Law of Unintended Consequences holds that the unforeseen and unanticipated consequences of well-intentioned social actions are always more important, and usually less agreeable, than the intended consequences. See David Whitman, "The Law of Welcome Surprises," *U. S. News and World Report*, December 30, 1996, 78.

11. Richard L. Stroup, "Newly Vulnerable to Superfund's Claws," *Wall Street Journal*, January 4, 1994, A-10. At one Superfund site, for example, the EPA was unsatisfied with contaminated dirt that everyone conceded was safe enough to eat for 70 days a year; it required $9.3 million of additional spending to clean the site to a level where the dirt would be safe enough to eat for 260 days a year.

12. Gordon Bishop, "Ruled Out: Cleanup Regulations Cost the State Jobs," *Newark Star Ledger*, June 21, 1993, 1.

13. Bishop, "Ruled Out," 1.

14. John D. Graham, "Regulations: A Risky Business," *Wall Street Journal*, May 18, 1994, A-14.

15. Data From: William A. McEachern, *Economics*, 3rd ed. Cincinnati, O.: South-

Western Publishing, 1994, 798.

16. Keith Bradsher, "The New Car Market's Lost Generation," *New York Times*, August 18, 1996, C-1.

17. "The Trouble with Trash," *U.S. News and World Report*, February 17, 1997, 14.

18. Tom Johnson, "Its System Banned by Court Rulings, State Plans Waste Disposal Changes," *Newark Star Ledger*, September 15, 1996, 17.

19. Diane C. Walsh, "Landfill Closing Sparks New Rush," *Newark Star Ledger*, December 8, 1996, 31.

20. Andy Newman, "Garbage Ruling Leaves the Counties in a $1.7 Billion Hole," *New York Times*, July 21, 1996, Sec. 13, 6.

21. Richard Schmalensee, "Green Costs and Benefits: The Buck Stops Where?" *Environment Strategy America*, 1994/1995, ed. By William K. Reilly, Hong Kong, Campden Publishing, 1994, 17.

Chapter 3
What Is Economics and
Why Study It?

The Need for Economics

Economics is always with us, to the consternation of many politicians, literary intellectuals, and even some environmentalists. Economics cannot be avoided because it is the process in all our lives — as individuals and societies — of providing for our material well-being.[1] If economics is the process of "how people earn their daily bread," it hardly seems to deserve its reputation as a tiresome and difficult subject. Yet "bread" is a complicated subject matter. Few people actually create their own bread, literally planting the seeds, raising the wheat, milling the flour, creating the yeast and other ingredients, and baking the resulting mixture. Most Americans, like the peoples of other economically advanced countries, never grow, raise, or hunt any significant share of the food they consume. Faced with the challenge of actually feeding ourselves, not to mention clothing ourselves and providing for our own shelter, electricity, heat, air conditioning, and transportation, most of us would be hopelessly ignorant and unprepared. Paradoxically, the more advanced is the society, the greater the inability of the average individual to survive alone and unaided without depending upon the efforts of others.

And, too, there never seems to be enough "bread," if by "bread" we mean all the goods and services we ordinarily need and want. In other words, we typically live under conditions of material scarcity. Economics can be viewed as the study of making choices under conditions of *scarcity*: Every individual, family, business firm, non-profit entity (like a college or a hospital), unit of government, and society faces the inescapable task of choosing among virtually limitless uses for its limited productive resources. In this sense, productive resources are always scarce since they are never adequate to satisfy all our needs and wants. Because scarcity is ever-present, it is a problem faced by the rich and poor alike. In the U. S., for example, even our vast wealth and huge annual production of goods and services (known as Gross Domestic Product or National Income) are woefully inadequate to satisfy all of our desires. Think of America's enormous unmet needs in the areas of healthcare and preventive medicine, nutrition, housing, day care, shelters, literacy and education, police protection, and public transportation, and our crumbling infrastructure of roads and bridges, not to mention the needs for environmental cleanup and pollution prevention. The persistent problem of annual U.S. federal government budget deficits underscores the difficulty of meeting a long list of programmatic wants and needs with limited economic resources, even though the federal government's revenues approach *$2 trillion* every year.

Economics often is formally defined as the study of how scarce productive resources are allocated among competing uses with the objective of maximizing some given goal or set of goals. The productive resources and goals can be those of an individual or a family, a profit-making business firm or a non-profit entity, an agency of government, or society as a whole. Economic analysis focuses achieving the greatest efficiency with which scarce productive resources can be used to achieve a given goal or set of goals. Economic rationality means choosing the least costly method for achieving goals through minimizing the use of scarce productive resources. The economically rational person, family, business, government, or society pursues many different ends simultaneously by carefully choosing among alternative goals and means in order to achieve the greatest total benefit consistent with its limited productive resources. Economics is *not* directly concerned with the choice of the ultimate goals themselves; rather, it deals with the best methods for attaining them. No mainstream economist would suggest, for example, that the value of environmental protection is a matter for economists to determine. Moreover, as we shall see, economists view environmental pollution and degradation as resulting from a flaw in the free market system, and therefore no economist would suggest that the level of environment protection is a matter for free markets to determine. However, most economists do strongly believe that the *market mechanism* can help to achieve a socially desired level of environmental protection most efficiently.

Because our world is one of limited productive resources, the resources available for environmental protection are necessarily limited. It makes economic sense, therefore, to concentrate society's productive resources where they accomplish the most environmental protection and remediation with the greatest efficiency. Evaluating environmental dangers based on good science, comparing the benefits of environmental protection and remediation against their costs, and using market-based strategies are desirable techniques precisely because they are pro-environmental techniques. Nor is it economically reasonable for society to pursue environmental protection in ways that work at cross purposes with promoting a healthy economy and the growth of jobs.

The Significance of Economics

Economics has long been distinguished from other fields of study by its subject matter and its methodology. However, the traditional boundary lines separating the various fields by subject matter have become less and less relevant in recent years. Nowadays, historians, political scientists, jurists and lawyers, sociologists, philosophers, psychologists, biologists and other natural scientists, architects, and engineers all discuss and debate the economic conditions of human life. By the same token, many economists now analyse arenas of human life previously thought to be essentially non-economic in nature, such as marriage and spouse selection; the bearing and raising of children; criminal behavior; cheating and lying; and, of course, politics, voting behavior, and electoral outcomes.

Economics is customarily subdivided into two major areas of study: *micro*economics (from the Greek for small, or micro) and *macro*economics (from the Greek for large, or macro). Microeconomics analyzes the behavior of individual economic units, like individuals, families, business firms, and industries. How costs and prices of particular goods, like apples or gasoline, are determined relates to microeconomics. As we will see, environmental economics is mainly microeconomics in nature. On the other hand, macroeconomics analyzes the functioning of the economy as a whole, like the determinants of Gross Domestic Product, inflation, and unemployment.

The Methodology of Economics

Because the subject matter boundaries among the different fields of inquiry have become so blurred as to be almost nonexistent, today it is primarily the *methodology* of economics that distinguishes it from other fields like history, political science, and philosophy. Just what is special about the methodology of economics? At least one difference between economics and the other disciplines is more apparent than real, namely the extensive use of mathematics in economics. Unfortunately, economists contribute to this misunderstanding by their frequent usage of equations, symbols, and complicated proofs, which helps obscure the underlying nature of economic analysis from the eyes of non-economist readers; few non-economists are willing to fight their way through intimidating jungles of mathematical obscurantism. But economics is *not* a discipline that rests on mathematics in any fundamental way, although mathematics can be a great convenience in developing theoretical propositions and communicating amongst economists themselves. Those not mathematically inclined should take heart: the two most influential books in the history of economic thought — Adam Smith's *The Wealth of Nations* and John Maynard Keynes' *The General Theory*, not to mention arguably the third most influential book in economic thought history, Alfred Marshall's *Principles of Economics* — contain hardly a single equation or any mathematics higher than fifth grade arithmetic.

Nonetheless, much of economics is fundamentally *quantitative* in nature, if not mathematical. The quantitative nature of economics has three important causes: one, economic analysis inherently makes many comparisons; two, economic analysis relies heavily on deductive logic in the use of economic models; and, three, economics is interested in predicting and empirically testing its predictions. Each of these reasons for the quantitative nature of economics can be briefly discussed.

The reason for comparison-making is rooted in the very nature of economics as the study of choice under conditions of scarcity. Almost any conceivable human endeavor — from taking a nap to bearing and raising a child to installing smoke-scrubbers on a polluting smokestack — conveys some benefit to somebody. But every human endeavor also requires the use of productive resources (also called by economists factors of production or inputs) for its achievement. Little more than a person's time is required for taking a nap, but much more complicated and varied productive resources are required to bear and raise a child, or to design, produce, and install smoke-scrubbers on smokestacks. Since available productive resources are always scarce relative to our needs and wants, all our needs and wants cannot be satisfied; that is, something must be given up in order to obtain something else. The "giving up" of some desired alternative is the essence of the economist's concept of opportunity cost. These arguments imply another form of comparison-making, namely pursuing an activity only up to the point where the extra benefit from it equals its extra cost, a logic that will be developed in detail in a later chapter.

Deductive Models

Although mathematics is not essential to economics methodology, the use of abstract, logically deductive models *is* fundamental to the economic approach. Economic analysis customarily proceeds from a beginning set of assumptions and proceeds to logically deduce conclusions, or outcomes. These conclusions can pertain to the activities of individuals, families, business firms, nonprofit organizations, industries, or even the performance of the economy as a whole. Deductive models are often expressed mathematically for the sake of convenience, but the use of mathematics as a means of expression should not be confused with the models themselves nor with the deductive process.

It is reasonable for a beginner to question why economic analysis depends on a methodology built on models and logical deduction. The answer lies in the greatest single fact about economic life: *the economic world is, for all practical purposes, infinitely complicated.* It is composed of hundreds of millions, even billions, of economic players, all constantly interacting with one another: Individual and family consumers; sellers of labor services; landlords and other property owners; capitalists (that is, the owners and sellers of the services of plant, equipment, and machinery); business firms, which employ the productive resources of others for the purpose of producing and selling goods in the marketplace; and governmental and quasi-governmental agencies and organizations, which also employ productive resources to create goods and deliver them either through the marketplace or outside normal market channels. In addition to the activities of all these economic players are the billions of prices to which their activities give rise: The prices of all the usual goods available in the marketplaces; the wage levels and salary rates for all the different types and varieties of labor; raw materials prices; land and housing prices and rents; stock and bond prices and interest rates; and on and on. Virtually all of these prices are constantly changing, often minute by minute or even second by second, under the impact of constantly changing decisions and activities by the economic players. The economy is nothing more or less than this flow of continuous activity and change. When our thinking expands to include international markets, which have become of major importance in economic life since World War II, the complexities involved in understanding the domestic economy are compounded by the addition of countless billions of transactions involving world trade.

The enormous complications of economic life are quite enough to endanger clear, accurate understanding, but history, politics, geography, climate, sociology, law, and psychology play their roles, too. The many influences over economic activity *never tell their own story.* It is only through developing and testing models, as Samuelson and Nordhaus remind us, that economists can seek to "simplify and organize the jumble of data and facts into a coherent view of reality."[2] In short, we need economic models and the deductive reasoning process to *simplify* the world. Economic models are merely the simplifications that permit economists to concentrate on the central features of a problem and eliminate the distractions of its less important features. It would *not* be a proper criticism of an economic model that some fact, or perhaps many facts, about the

Across the Disciplines:
Positive vs. Normative Thinking

Over thirty years ago the English writer C.P. Snow shocked the intellectual world with his disturbing "two cultures" thesis, which described western society as "increasingly being split into two polar groups."[1] The polarization Snow suggested is a frighteningly wide chasm between, on the one hand, the culture of the "literary intellectuals," including philosophers, historians, and people in the arts and, on the other hand, the culture of the "scientists," including applied scientists, engineers, and the like. Each group maintains its own recognizable common attitudes, standards, patterns of behavior, approaches, and assumptions, which are quite distinct from those of the other group.

The problem for the larger society, Snow argued, is not merely the fact that the two cultures exist side-by-side, at separate tables it were, but that almost no communication or understanding passes between them. Each is unsympathetic and often uninterested, unaware, or even hostile to the activities and mental processes of the other group. A recent illustration of this lack of awareness was the first proposed *National History Standards for United States History, Grades 5-12*, which dozens of nationally recognized historians labored for three years to produce. These Standards totally omitted any mention of the role and importance of science in contemporary life. "How is it possible," two scientists, Robert Park and Ursula Goodenough, complained, "to view the 20th century without noticing science? Electricity, radio, jet travel, weather satellites, nuclear energy, antibiotics, the genetic code, the eradication of smallpox, the Apollo moon landing, and the cyber revolution might as well have dropped from the sky."[2]

One of the central differences between literary intellectuals and scientists, to use Snow's terms, is the perspective each brings to the act of observation. In many ways, these perspectives are opposites to each other. The literary intellectual accumulates detail, makes much of seeming irrelevancies, uses the simplest of events — a polluted creek downstream from a box-making factory — as the occasion for the most elaborate of descriptions and implications. The scientist, on the other hand, does not so much seek to accumulate facts as to distill them. The scientifically oriented investigator must *actively resist* the tug of those rich, very effusive descriptions of reality, discarding them in favor of the abstract and the general: not this *particular* creek, on this day, in this light, near this factory making this product, but a *general* problem of, say, lack of ownership rights, negative externalities, and market failure, resulting in the transmission of faulty price signals to producers and consumers, their effects neatly plotted by curves or described by a symbolic formula.

Another way of expressing what separates the two cultures is the relative importance each places on positive and normative thinking. Positive statements seek to address factual or predictive propositions about what is and what if. Normative statements, in contrast, involve ethical precepts, subjective perspectives, and value judgments. Economics, like the modern natural sciences, depends largely on the use of positive statements and analysis. This orientation toward the positive is reflected in its use of the scientific method, deductive logic, quantitative data, and empirical analysis to understand problems and explain behavior.

Distinguishing between positive and normative statements always involves the difference between observing, measuring, or predicting an event (positive) versus making subjective or ethical evaluations about the event (normative). For example, "if the price of gasoline rises consumers will purchase less of it (all other determinants of gasoline demand being constant)" is a positive statement. On the other hand, "Consumers should be more sensitive to the problem of air pollution caused by burning gasoline

and should purchase less gasoline for the sake of achieving cleaner air" is a normative statement. The positive statement expresses some objective reality *without regard to the personal viewpoint of the individual speaker*, while any normative statement always includes a subjective perspective by the speaker. For most mainstream economists, the distinction between subjective normative judgment and testable positive analysis is the difference, in the words of MIT economist Paul Krugman, "between the essentially literary sensibility that we expect of a card-carrying intellectual and the scientific-mathematical outlook that is arguably the true glory of our civilization."[3]

Notes

1. C.P. Snow, *The Two Cultures: And a Second Look*, 2nd edition, New York, The New American Library, 1963, 11.

2. R.L. Park and V. Goodenough, "The Unmaking of American Science Policy: The End of the Scientific Era?," *Academe*, 82, 1996,15.

3. Quoted by Louis Uchitelle, "Like Oil and Water: A Tale of Two Economists," *New York Times*, February 16, 1997, Sec.3, 1.

real world were omitted from the analysis. If every fact about a problem were included, the result would not be a model but a description of reality itself, and the economist would be overwhelmed by a torrent of facts. On the other hand, it would be a proper criticism of an economic model if, in the quest for simplification, the analysis had omitted an essential feature about the problem at hand.

How would we know if an essential aspect of the problem had been wrongly omitted from the analysis? The answer lies in the ability of a model to predict outcomes and behavior. Accurate prediction, within reasonable boundaries, is the final arbiter of solid economic analysis. If an economic theory regularly makes reasonably accurate predictions — no matter how simple its formulation — it passes the essential test. If a theory does not make reasonably accurate predictions — no matter how elegant its theoretical formulation — it must be rejected. An example of the ability of economics to successfully predict is shown by a famous bet made in 1980. The bet occurred between an economist, Julian L. Simon, and a prominent ecologist, Paul Ehrlich, the best-selling author of *The Population Bomb*. The substance of their bet is presented in the accompanying information box: *An Economist and an Ecologist Make a Wager*.

The Scientific Method

As in the natural sciences, model-building in economics entails carefully working through a series of calculated steps. These steps are sometimes called the *scientific method*. This methodology proceeds in seven phases:

Phase 1. Define the Problem.

First of all, a scientific problem must be defined in a scientifically useful way. To reduce the amount of nitrous oxide level by x hundreds of thousands of tons in a given five county area is a manageable task, while "protecting the environment" or "enhancing environmental quality" are not scientifically manageable tasks. Obviously, we hope to achieve the latter by accomplishing the former: that is the whole point of a nitrous oxide reduction program. But the former is a scientifically manageable problem that can be measured, analyzed, and dealt with through a variety of means, while the latter is too broad in its formulation to lend itself to any deliberate, measurable, scientific remedy.

An Economist and an Ecologist Make a Wager[1]

One of the methodological strengths of mainstream neoclassical economics is its ability to make good predictions in comparison to the less scientific, normatively oriented fields of study. The predictive ability of economics was actually put to an interesting test in a well known bet in 1980 between a world-famous ecologist and an economist. The economist was Julian L. Simon of the University of Maryland and the ecologist was Paul Ehrlich, whose 1968 book, *The Population Bomb*, sold over three million copies. Ehrlich has been a leading spokesman for the view that the earth is running out of available land and resources because of a growing world population and the rising level of industrial and agricultural production necessary to sustain it. Actually, Ehrlich's core idea — that the planet is rapidly reaching its carrying capacity with resulting land, food, raw materials, and energy shortages — is a very old belief. It is essentially the same idea popularized two hundred years ago by Parson Malthus (hence the term "Malthusian") in his *Essays on the Principle of Population* (1798). Malthus believed that the growing number of mouths to feed must inevitably exceed the earth's ability to feed them. The same basic Malthusian idea, this time in the form of computerized projections and trend lines, received wide publicity in *The Limits to Growth*

(1972), written by Donella Meadows and others, a book which one prominent mainstream economist, William Nordhaus, characterized as having been written by "Chicken Little with a computer."[2]

Malthusian predictions are constructed on the assumption that current production and consumption practices and technologies will remain essentially unchanged and unchecked. Neoclassical economics, on the other hand, holds that these things change — sometimes dramatically — in response to shifting opportunities, circumstances, shortages, and surpluses. In other words, scarcities of oil, minerals, food, land, or any other productive resource cause their prices to rise (relative to the prices of other resources), encouraging rational users to substitute away from the now-more expensive resources toward now-cheaper alternatives. Needless to say, the results can lead to sweeping and profound changes in human behavior, quite independent of emotional exhortations and "consciousness raising" efforts by well-intentioned Malthusians.

For Simon, the economist, the trouble with Ehrlich's doom-and-gloom scenario was that the expected warning signs were virtually nonexistent: If the earth actually were reaching its limits to growth because of land or food or mineral or energy shortages, there should be telltale rising prices of land, food, minerals, and energy. In actuality, Simon knew that heses prices had been *declining* relative to labor's wages for two centuries and especially so in the yeasr just prior to 1980. Price declines had even occurred despite sharply expanding world population and industrial production levels. In fact, technological advances had made food much more abudnant and falling grain prices had contributed to rising nutritional standards throughout much of the much world.

Simon challenged Ehrlich in 1980 to a unique wager: Ehrlich could choose any five resources that he believed would become more scarce over the next ten years, as measured by their market price increase between 1980 and 1990 (less an adjustment for general inflation). Simon was willing to bet that Ehrlich's five resources would become less scarce over the next ten years, as measured by their market price decline. Ehrlich chose $200 worth of five different metals he felt most certain to become scarcer over the next ten years. Then they waited ten years to see how much the same physical quantities of these metals cost in 1990. The data are shown in the following table:

Physical Quantities Purchased	Ehrlich's Selected Metals	Cost in 1980	Cost in 1990 (adjusted for general inflation)
196.6 lbs	Copper	$200	$163
51.3 lbs	Chrome	200	120
65.3 lbs	Nickel	200	193
229.1 lbs	Tin	200	56
13.6 lbs	Tungsten	200	86
		====	====
		$1,000	$618

Ehrlich's five metals bought for $1,000 in 1980 could have been purchased in 1990 (after adjusting for general inflation) for only $618! This astonishing result was all the more remarkable since Ehrlich had selected five resources he thought were in most crucial short supply and therefore the most likely to go up in price. The lesson of this story is to never underestimate human and technological adaptability. Human beings are suprisingly flexible, proving over thousands of years how capable they are of making appropriate changes when changes are needed. A market economy can be viewed as a cultural artifact that facilitates and extends the possibilities for human adaptability: When we run low on one resource, markets signal that new substitutes must be found or created — fiber optic lines and space satellites in place of telephone lines that once used only copper wire; high-tech ceramics instead of tungsten in cutting tools. The substitution of aluminum for tin in cans and containers was encouraged when the price of tin rose, and the substitution of plastic for aluminum when the price of aluminum rose. The current technological changes toward miniaturization promise to conserve even more of countless different resources.

In summary, the general outlook of Simon and most neoclassical economists is one of *optimism*, based on technological change and an efficient system of markets. This viewpoint is in sharp contrast to the *pessimism* of Ehrlich, Meadows, and other Malthusian ecologists, who envision an inexorable depletion of natural resources and available land accompanying the growth of world population and production.

Notes

1. The basic facts about the Simon-Ehrlich wager were reported by John Tierney, "Betting the Planet," *New York Times Sunday Magazine*, December 2, 1990.
2. William D. Nordhaus, "A Review of Joel E. Cohen, How Many People Can the Earth Support," in *New York Times Review of Books*, January 14, 1996, 12.

Phase 2. Observe the relevant facts.

This step is especially tricky because it requires knowing which facts about a problem are most important, which are less important, and which only tangentially related. A theoretical understanding of economics and some knowledge about the immediate problem at hand primarily inform these choices. Success in this area is commonly called "having a feel" for a problem, and it is typically based on solid theoretical as well as trial-and-error field experience.

Phase 3. Develop Simplifying Assumptions.

A well-planned and executed observation of the relevant facts surrounding the problem leads to the creation of a simplifying set of assumptions on which the analysis can operate. This step requires that the researcher must accept a degree of abstraction to help in "seeing" the problem. Without creating abstractions, models cannot exist. It may be true that "everything counts" and "everything depends on everything else," but no sensible hypothesis can be formulated or scientifically tested under such a lack of theoretical restriction.

Phase 4. Formulate the Hypothesis.

Based on observation of the relevant facts and the creation of assumptions about economic behavior, it is possible to postulate a testable hypothesis (or several hypotheses). The hypothesis presumes that certain stable relationships exist. An example would be that, based on the assumptions that consumers are rational and act to maximize their own individual economic welfare, consumers will buy and consume less gasoline when the price per gallon rises, holding constant the other major determinants of gasoline demand. It could be additionally hypothesized that the longer the time period under consideration, the stronger would be the negative effect of gasoline price increases on gasoline consumption. Finally, based on the same assumptions about economically rational consumer behavior, it also could be hypothesized that a decrease in the price of goods that consumers can substitute for driving their own cars (e.g., taxi fares, bus fares, or the wait-time for buses, which is also a cost to the consumer) would reduce consumers' demand for gasoline.

Phase 5. Test the Predictions.

To be useful in a scientific sense, a model must be testable. It must be "seen in action" to determine if it helps explain the problem the researcher is trying to understand. A helpful model must give predictable results that shed light on how the real world works. It bears emphasis that the economist is not predicting how the world *should* work, or the *morally best* way for it to work, or the most *politically appealing* solution. The economist is concerned with helping explain what actually occurs, even if it is personally unpleasant or morally abhorrent. The preceding three propositions relating to the relationship between gasoline consumption, gasoline prices, and the prices of substitute goods for gasoline are predictions that can all be tested with real data, regardless of the researcher's personal views about, say, the desirability of consumers driving private automobiles and its impact on the environment.

Phase 6. Evaluate the Results.

As with any scientific field, a theory is useful only when it serves to predict and these predicted results explain how the real world works. Evaluation of results requires a systematic comparison of predictions with available data. Applying statistical analysis to economic data sometimes can require advanced tools in probability and econometrics, which is the blending of economics and statistics. But understanding the analytical results requires only careful reading, common sense, and an open mind.

Phase 7. Accept or Reject the Model.

A "successful" economic theory is one that has survived much testing and has become part of the working system of mainstream economics. For example, if the last ten times gasoline prices increased in a given market area consumers reduced their consumption of gasoline (holding constant the determinants of gasoline demand except its price), then one has good evidence for accepting the hypothesis that gasoline prices and gasoline demand are inversely related. If the last ten times bus fares increased in a given market area consumers increased their demand for gasoline (holding constant the determinants of gasoline demand except bus fares), this is good evidence for accepting the hypothesis that gasoline demand and the prices of substitute goods are positively related.

Most beginning students are surprised to learn that a theory can never be finally, irrevocably proven. No amount of successful testing of a theory can ever prove it. However, contradictory evidence can lead to rejecting a bad theory. Thus, it has been said that a good theory is only a theory that has not yet been rejected. Nothing is more essential to a scientific theory than that it makes accurate predictions, showing that it *helps* explain how the real world works. But accuracy in predicting and explaining, at best, only means limited wrongness. An economic model, or even an elaborate theoretical doctrine, is best understood as conveying the basic idea that economics is attempting to understand behavior and, in this attempt, a partial examination is better than none at all or many wrong explanations.[3]

Economics as Thought Processing

Economic analysis is a distinctive "way of thinking" about problems rather than a set of pre-digested answers waiting to be taken off the shelf. This special way of thinking is related to psychologist Dawes' idea that thinking is the creation of mental representations about what is *not* directly before our eyes in viewing the world. He maintains that observing a green wall in front of our eyes is *not* an example of thinking. However, imagining what that wall would look like if it were repainted blue *is* thinking.[4] Dawes' view closely corresponds with the idea of Bartlett, one of the founders of the field of cognitive psychology. Bartlett understood thinking as a skill that intimately involves us in filling in the gaps in our factual evidence.[5] To both Dawes and Bartlett, thinking is a matter of making up through mental effort for the deficiencies in data we do not possess (and often can never possess). The connection between the mental skill in filling in the gaps in our data and the nature of economic analysis becomes even clearer with Dawes' further sub-division of thinking into "lower-level" and "higher-level" thought processes. The former he terms "automatic" thinking, the latter "controlled" thinking. Lower level, or automatic, thinking is usually associational: Something we see in our environment simply brings an idea to mind. On the other hand, higher level, or controlled, thinking is abstract and hypothetical, which are the essential qualities required for model-building.

To help see the difference between simpler automatic thinking and more complicated controlled thinking, refer to the earlier discussion about gasoline demand. Many non-economists argue that individuals do not buy less gasoline when gasoline prices rise. "People just don't behave that way," they might argue, "despite what economic theory says. One thing about gasoline is that when your tank is empty you drive to the service station and fill-up. You can't park your car because the price of gasoline is up a few cents a gallon. You fill-up and pay the price, regardless." How does this person know that? For one thing, the person probably has filled-up his or her tank many hundreds of times and not once driven away with an empty tank after seeing that gasoline prices had increased. The image (or representation, or idea) of what constitutes gasoline demand is "automatically" associated with one's own experiences in filling-up. This person never drove away from the service station without buying gasoline, so there is no relationship between a higher gasoline price and reduced quantity. The conclusion, Dawes would say, is "automatic."

"Controlled" thinking shows several logical flaws in this conclusion. For one thing, there possibly could be other buyers who, in fact, do buy less gasoline at higher prices, but they do not happen to be personal acquaintances. Consequently, one's first-hand experiences, even hundreds of them, can be irrelevant for determining whether higher gasoline prices actually reduce the quantity purchased. But more importantly, the inverse relationship between gasoline prices and quantities purchased *usually requires some time to develop* as consumers change behavior and search for cheaper substitute goods. The inverse price-quantity relationship is greater the longer the time period under consideration. Casual, non-scientific observation can be easily misled because of the length of time that often separates a causal event (higher gasoline prices) from its final economic effect (less gasoline purchased). *In between the initial cause and the final effect occur numerous behavioral modifications and ad-*

justments by economically rational consumers: more bus riding, more car pooling, fewer Sunday drives in the country, relocating closer to work, more flex-time at work (e.g., four day-weeks), and purchasing more fuel-efficient cars, all of which reduce the quantity of gasoline purchased.

Notes

1. Robert L. Heilbroner, *The Making of Economic Society*, Englewood Cliffs, NJ, Prentice-Hall, 1985.
2. Paul Samuelson and William D. Nordhaus, *Economics*, 14th edition, New York, McGraw-Hill, 1992, 4.
3. George J. Stigler, "The Successes and Failures of Professor Smith," *The Journal of Political Economy*, 84,6, 1211.
4. Richard Dawes, *Rational Choice in an Uncertain World*, New York, Harcourt, Brace, Jovanovich, 1988, 3.
5. Frank Bartlett, *Thinking: An Experimental and Social Study*, New York, Basic Books, 1958, 4.

Chapter 4
Economic Systems and the Environment

In Chapter Three we saw that economics is an inescapable part of our everyday lives. Economics is always with us because it deals with a process every individual and society must confront — the need to provide for our material well-being. Ensuring that material wants and needs are provided for actually involves several separate economic tasks. *Every society*, whether modern or traditional, democratic or totalitarian, rich or poor, *must answer four fundamental economic questions*: (1) *What* goods to produce? (2) *How* to produce them? (3) *Who* among the members of society is to receive these goods? (4) *How much* of these goods are they to receive?

Three Organizational Systems

How these basic production and income distribution tasks are managed goes to the very core of any society. Remarkably, over the sweep of all human history mankind has effectively managed these tasks in very few ways. Despite an enormous diversity of local political and cultural variations that have shaped daily economic life, *only three archetypes of systems exist* that, separately or in combination, enable societies to solve their basic economic tasks. These three great archetypal organizational forms are (1) custom and tradition, (2) command-and-control, and (3) the market system with voluntary exchange.

Custom and Tradition

By any measure of human history, custom and tradition is an ancient archetypal system. Essentially, it solves the basic economic tasks by endlessly reiterating the jobs, techniques, assignments, and rewards of the past. Social and political institutions frequently are grounded on unchanging, rigid ideas about status, rank, and occupation, which often are determined at the time of a person's birth. In our own Western culture, the hereditary allocation of jobs and status was one of society's main stabilizing forces during the Middle Ages and beyond, extending into the sixteenth, seventeenth, and even eighteenth centuries. In less modernized and economically developed parts of the world, the power of custom and tradition to govern what to produce, how to produce it, and who should get how much remains strong to the present day.

Command-and-Control

The second organizational system for managing society's basic economic tasks also boasts an ancient lineage. This is the method of authority imposed from above, of command-and-control. Under this system, economic outcomes depend on decisions, rewards, and punishments passed down from a higher authority. Persuasion and voluntary compliance are *not* central features of getting society's necessary economic tasks accomplished under command-and-control. In its political form, command-and-control can range from extreme totalitarianism to mild authoritarianism within an otherwise democratic political context.

An example of a strongly authoritarian command-and-control system was precapitalist mercantilism in Europe: A complicated network of subsidies, special privileges, patents, grants of monopoly, tariffs and other taxes, navigation laws, and trade restrictions through which the European governments of the sixteenth, seventeenth, and eighteenth centuries sought to encourage nationalism, national self-sufficiency, and national power. It was largely a series of bitter conflicts over England's mercantilistic interferences with the American colonies' freedom of commerce and industry that led to the American rebellion against the English Crown and the promulgation of the Declaration of Independence in 1776. Totalitarian examples of command-and-control were the centralized planning systems of the now-defunct Soviet Union and the Eastern European nations under Communist Party rule, as well as the crumbling economy of Castro's Cuba. The dominant form of environmental protection in the U. S. today provides an example of mild authoritarian command-and-control operating within the broader context of political democracy. As we saw in Chapter Two, the essence of this approach is an enormously complicated, top-to-bottom patchwork of government standards, mandates, and regulations.

From the precapitalist European mercantilistic policies to the central planning practices of the former Soviet Union, Eastern Bloc countries, and Cuba to most current U. S. environmental regulations, command-and-control systems typically engender gross economic inefficiencies. Sometimes these inefficiencies arise because governments are simply unable to organize and manage productive resources to achieve their stated objectives at reasonable cost, becoming mired in ever expanding bureaucratic requirements, rules, and regulations. But the most serious command-and-control inefficiencies are more subtle than an obvious system breakdown or failure to achieve an objective. Indeed, command-and-control organization can be very effective in attaining a *single-purpose* objective, like building the pyramids of ancient Egypt or the Great Wall of China or the spectacular cathedrals of medieval Europe or the heavy industrial factories of Stalin's U.S.S.R. in the 1930s and 1940s. Moreover, almost all governments resort to highly coercive, authoritarian command-and-control practices to marshall a nation's economic resources to fight wars. Examples of such coercive practices are drafting people into the military; requisitioning private property, with or without payment; imposing curbs on the use of private property; forbidding certain foreign trading; and limiting the types and amounts of goods people can buy through rationing and other limitations on consumers.

Aside from the loss of individual freedoms and liberal values, the major sources of command-and-control inefficiencies are the distortions imposed on all other economic activities when goals and objectives are ignored other than those approved by the higher authorities. Regulation via command-and-control usually treats one objective as categorically more important than all other ends: for example, elevating environmental protection over other considerations having to do with, say, consumer convenience, cost, product availability and selection, or jobs creation. Diverting society's scarce productive resources toward *any* goal selected by higher authorities inevitably interferes with achieving all other private and social goals. Thus, command-and-control often disregards the need to trade-off the partial achievement of one goal for the partial achievement of others. Economic efficiency, on the other hand, requires carefully balancing one goal against all others, including private and public consumption and investment activities, economic growth, and employment creation.

The Market System

A third way for society to solve its basic tasks of production and income distribution is a market system organized around voluntary exchange. As a primary means for organizing economic activity, the market system first evolved in western Europe scarcely 250 years ago. Because the market economy is far and away the newest and the most elusive to comprehend of the three archetypal systems, it is also the least understood and the most maligned. The market system is especially difficult to grasp because *it is the only organizational form in which order, efficiency, and social improvement emerge, apparently spontaneously, out of individual selfishness and the appearance of social disorder.*

The first writer to systematically describe the benefits of a market system organized around voluntary exchange was Adam Smith. He accomplished this feat in one of the most important books in the history of western civilization, *An Inquiry into the Nature and Causes of the Wealth of Nations*, or *The Wealth of Nations* for short. Published in 1776, Smith's book added to the signing of America's Declaration of Independence a second profoundly revolutionary event in that momentous year. Like most great works, *The Wealth of Nations* was the product of both the man and his times. It was clearly inspired by Smith's philosophical predecessors — men like John Locke, William Petty, Bernard de Mandeville, Anne-Robert Turgot, Richard Cantillon, Francois Quesnay, and especially David Hume — in the then-newly emerging body of western liberal thought. Smith drew freely on all of them to help answer the major political-philosophical question of his day (and ours): Can social order and improvement emerge out of the potential chaos and anarchy of an individualistic society? Can a society in which everyone busily pursues his or her own self-interest accomplish the basic economic tasks necessary for its survival if no higher authority imposes its commands from above? These questions led Smith to *visualize* a new structure of economic life, organized around a system of free markets that determine prices, production, and employment through voluntary cooperation. Relying on the pursuit of individual self-interest, Smith's economic vision saw operating an "invisible hand," as he called it; through this powerful but unseen force, individuals' "regard to their own interest [and] their self-love" create outcomes that are "most agreeable to the interest of the whole society."

The many advancements in economic theory in the 225 years since *The Wealth of Nations* have come to form an integrated body of mainstream economic doctrine. All the major figures in the development of mainstream economic thought — from David Ricardo and John Stuart Mill in the early and mid-nineteenth century; to Stanley Jevons and Alfred Marshall in the late nineteenth century; A.C. Pigou, Frank Knight, and John R. Hicks in the early twentieth century; and finally Milton Friedman, Kenneth Arrow, George Stigler, and James N. Buchanan in the mid-twentieth century — have contributed, each in his own special way, to a coherent, integrated system of thought. This mainstream of economic analysis is today often called *neoclassical theory*. The best way to appreciate the genius of these thinkers is to examine their collective description of what a market system is and how it works.

Economic theory maintains that a system of decentralized markets, organized around voluntary exchange and motivated by the pursuit of individual self-interest, provides the best answers to society's production and income distribution problems. It does so for three basic reasons: *One,* a decentralized market system with voluntary exchange complements a liberal democratic body politic in which personal freedoms and individual liberties are protected to the greatest extent possible; individuals are free to pursue their own goals as they see fit with a minimum of outside coercion. *Two,* a market system enjoys the benefits of large numbers of individual decision-makers (producers, consumers, and sellers of productive services). *Three,* a market system usually sends the proper set of price "signals." These prices, in effect, are incentives to producers, consumers, and sellers of productive services, guiding them toward their most efficient uses. Productive services include the services of labor, land and natural resources, and capital. In a market system, these productive services are "sold" to producers, who employ them for the purpose of producing goods.

In the pursuit of its own self-interest, each seller of a productive service and each business seeks to sell its productive service or good for as much as possible, while the competition that each imposes on the behavior of all others limits the possibilities for price, wage, rent, and profit increases. In the case of labor, for example, the more employers there are, the greater are the choices that workers possess; the impersonal forces of competition among employers for workers protect their interests. Competition and freedom of choice among workers together with competition and freedom of enterprise among producers generally lead firms to produce what consumers want at the lowest possible production costs.

As the wants and tastes of consumers change, changing price signals cause productive resources to move from lower-valued activities to higher-valued ones. The market's responsiveness and flexibility does not rely on the good will or humane intentions of individual employers, workers or sellers of other productive resources, nor upon the wisdom of political leaders. The market system yields its generally excellent results even if employers, workers and other sellers of productive resources, and political leaders are unwise, greedy, or purely selfish. The market winnows out the follies of its individual participants and plays the greed and selfishness of some against the greed and selfishness of others. This is surely one way of understanding the meaning of Adam Smith's "invisible hand." As a general rule, a system of competitive free markets organized around voluntary exchange responds to individual and social wants with the greatest possible efficiency. *The primary exception to the general rule relates to "market failure" because of the existence of "negative externalities." As we shall see in Chapter Six, when "negative externalities" exist private consumers may not allocate their expenditures and producers may not operate their plants and factories in ways that maximize social welfare.*

The Evolution of Environmental Economics

Environmental economics is a relatively new specialization within the field of economics, essentially dating only from the 1960s when, in response to widely expressed environmental concerns, the discipline began taking quality-of-life issues much more seriously than in the simpler days before environmental awareness. As we have seen, the development of mainstream economic theory since Adam Smith was a collective enterprise. Because of several earlier theoretical developments — one of them dating from the nineteenth century — the mainstream of neoclassical economics was remarkably well-prepared to adapt to the new concern over environmental issues. Two men in particular — Vilfredo Pareto and Arthur Cecil Pigou — stand out for their special accomplishments in dealing with the problems of economic efficiency and externalities, the theoretical cornerstones on which modern environmental economics is constructed.

Pareto and Efficiency

The first of the two men, Vilfredo Pareto, an Italian born in Paris who taught at Lausanne University, Switzerland, gave mainstream economics its definition for that which it prizes above all else: *efficiency*. So long as it is possible to reallocate economic resources in some way to make a person (or a group) better off — in the sense that they would prefer the new situation over the original situation — while at the same time making no one else worse off, the existing pattern of resource allocation is not efficient. A situation in which it is impossible to make anyone better off without making someone else worse off is technically known as "Pareto efficient" or "Pareto optimal." Modern-day welfare economics is largely concerned with attempting to establish the necessary conditions that must be fulfilled to achieve a Pareto efficient allocation of resources.

In a modern society, almost any conceivable new legislation or any change in policy that government might implement would make someone worse off, thereby failing the Pareto efficiency test. But if the benefits from a proposed legislative or policy change were large enough for the winners to compensate the losers, the change could be feasibly accomplished, moving society in the direction of a Pareto-efficient allocation of its resources. A criterion for policy-making consistent with Pareto efficiency would be to require that the winners from a policy change fully compensate from their gains the losers from the same change. The losers would be considered fully compensated if they preferred their new situation over their original one (or were indifferent as between the second and the first). The primary advantage of Pareto efficient public policies is that they maximize society's total economic output within the limits of its current resource base and distribution of income. A reallocation of resources toward Pareto efficiency is a win-win situation. As one example, a Pareto efficient change might occur if the government of California were to rearrange the state's water rights. At present, farmland in semiarid California comes endowed with legal rights to a percentage of water from a given reservoir, and the price farmers pay for the water is about $10 per acre-foot. At the same time, water for city use is priced ten times higher, $100 per acre-foot. Such a low price for agricultural water has resulted in such clearly socially inefficient, but nevertheless privately profitable, uses of water as growing irrigated hay in Death Valley.[1] The practice of granting farmers entitlements to water at $10 per acre foot is economically inefficient because it reduces the size of California's total economic output below what it would be if some of the water could be used by a producer outside of agriculture, say, in manufacturing, in order to expand industrial output in California.

A movement toward Pareto optimality seems very feasible in this example: If the state government transferred agricultural water to other productive sectors in need of the water, the state could generate enough additional tax money to fully compensate the farmers for their reduced production *and* have money left over to fund other environmental protection activities, a general tax cut for all Californians, or some third alternative. One study, cited by Goodstein, estimated that California's total economic output would rise by $5 billion if only its water were allocated efficiently.[2] Raising the price of water to its free market level, say $70 per acre-foot, was attempted in a 1982 statewide initiative, but it was defeated at the polls due to strong farmer opposition. However, merely raising the price of water would *not* have been Pareto efficient, since it would have left farmers clearly worse off. But a Pareto-improving policy is theoretically possible that could make California farmers equally well off, or better off, while making other productive sectors better off and raising the state's total output. The Pareto improvement involves the use of market-based reforms for water usage. Farmers would be allowed to continue to purchase their water allotments at the old price of $10 per acre-foot, but then they would be allowed to resell them to the highest bidder. "In this case, the Death Valley farmer could continue to grow hay but, by doing so, would be passing up substantial profit opportunities. By simply reselling the water the farmer could make $90 per acre-foot!"[3] Non-agricultural producers would benefit by having the ability to purchase needed water at market prices.

The Principle of Compensation

The idea of Pareto efficiency leads to a broad principle in mainstream economics, the Principle of Compensation. When society asks its members — individual consumers, property owners, or producers — to bear the burden of an activity that benefits society as a whole, then the individual is owed compensation from the rest of society. There is a long tradition, in this country as well as others, of compensation for physical property taken in eminent domain proceedings. However, past practice and conceptual thinking must be greatly broadened, particularly in the environmental area. When society wants to take a positive action that adds to net social welfare, like creating open space, then society should pay for that open space "rather than stopping someone from developing their property and essentially forcing them to provide a public park at private expense."[4] Regulatory actions that reduce private property values are called "takings," as when land-use controls deprive private owners of the use of their property for all practical purposes as much as outright seizure, but without eminent domain compensation — leaving the private owners to bear the cost of providing social benefits, like waterfront access or undeveloped open space, that should be borne by society at large.[5]

A recent U.S. Supreme Court ruling greatly expanded the potential for the protection of private property against "takings" in an important legal case. During a 1992 drought in southern Oregon and northern California, Oregon's Fish and Wildlife Service cut-off irrigation water to farms and ranches near Oregon's Lost River. The irrigation water cut-off was done under the Endangered Species Act to maintain higher water levels in two reservoirs to protect the habitat of two endangered species of fish. As a result of the irrigation water cut-off, however, ranchers and farmers in the area suffered an estimated $75 million in losses and damages. Two Oregon ranchers and two irrigation districts sued over the government's enforcement of the Endangered Species Act, alleging that there was no evidence that the population of the two endangered species of fish was declining in the reservoirs or that higher water levels would help the fish. Lower courts previously had ruled that only private parties claiming *underenforcement* of the Act had legal standing to sue over how the federal law was enforced, and that private parties claiming economic damage as a result of *overenforcement* of the Act did not have the ability to sue over enforcement issues. In March, 1997, the Supreme Court unanimously overruled the lower courts, in effect allowing private parties who claim to have suffered economic harm from enforcement of the Act to invoke the same Act against the government. Most other Federal environmental laws — including the Clean Water Act, the Clean Air Act, the Safe Drinking Water Act, and others — also include "citizen suit" provisions that will presumably now be available to those seeking to challenge regulatory overenforcement as well as regulatory underenforcement under those laws.

Some other recent environmental examples of the Principle of Compensation are:

☐ When the states of New York and New Jersey decided that 15,800 acres of forests, meadows, lakes, and streams along their joint border (— the so-called Sterling Forest —) should be preserved in perpetuity to safeguard a major watershed for drinking water, they joined with the federal government to purchase the ecosystem with public monies rather than prohibit, through land-use controls, a planned massive residential, commercial, and industrial development on the property.

☐ The same federal government legislation that helped finance the Sterling Forest purchase also helped finance a 180-acre Tallgrass Prairie National Preserve in Kansas; a 25,800-acre Opal Creek Wilderness and National Scenic Recreation Area in Oregon; protection for 51 miles of the Columbia River in Washington state and 11.5 miles of the Maprey River in New Hampshire; and the U.S. Department of the Interior's acquisition of 275,000 acres of oil and gas development rights owned by a private producer in two national wildlife refuges and a park on the Alaska Peninsula.

☐ The state of California and the federal government collaborated to avert the logging of ancient redwood trees through the purchase of two redwood groves of about 3,500 acres. A tract of land connecting them and a buffer around it all were also purchased to help protect wildlife and fish in the area.

☐ The Trust for Public Land has spent over $1 billion to purchase available private land for either resale or transfer to various environmental groups, state governments, and the U.S. Park Service, for the purpose of keeping the land undeveloped forever.

The Compensation Principle has even broader environmental implications than these examples suggest. Some poor countries that want to develop are burning off their rain forests at a very rapid rate, thereby contributing to an increase in the atmospheric content of greenhouse gases. The chief offender is Brazil, where the burning of the Amazon forests emitted 1,100,000 thousand metric tons of carbon dioxide in 1992. The original climate-change treaty signed at the Earth Summit in Rio de Janeiro in 1992 has done little or nothing to slow forest-burning by Brazil and other developing countries. The dilemma is that poverty and resource scarcity in these poor countries have led them to prefer a less clean environment in their pursuit of economic development.[6] They are not as willing to pay for a clean environment as, say, Americans are willing to pay, nor are they willing to dedicate their forests to serve as "the lungs of the world" for the primary benefit of others. According to the Principle of Compensation, it could be appropriate for richer countries to pay poorer countries to reduce forest clearing and greenhouse gas emissions that benefit everyone. In fact, the United States has already proposed that the United Nations begin developing such a compensation plan.[7]

Pigou and Externalities

Arthur Cecil Pigou's predecessor in the Chair of Political Economy at Cambridge University had been Alfred Marshall. From Marshall's famous *Principles of Economics* Pigou learned that an external effect, or externality, in consumption exists when the consumption of a good by one person has a direct effect, positive or negative, on the welfare of another person *and* this effect is not contained in the price of the good paid by the first consumer. Similarly, an externality in production occurs when the production activities of one producer directly effect, positively or negatively, the activities of another producer *and* this effect is excluded from the price of the good charged by the first producer. The essence of an externality, whether in consumption or production, is that some cost or benefit is not accurately reflected in the market price of a good. Because the externality is not reflected in the market price of a good, the individual consumer or producer responsible for creating the externality fails to take its effect on others into account. An example of a *negative consumption externality* occurs when, for example, Smith, wanting privacy, builds a wall on his property that reduces the amount of sunshine flooding into Jone's window, assuming Jones likes sunshine. If Jones detests sunshine, then Smith's wall creates a *positive consumption externality* for Jones. An example of a *negative production externality* occurs when Upstream Chemical Co. discharges effluent into a river, which increases the production costs of Downstream Beverages Co. farther down the river. A *positive production externality* arises when Upstream Chemical Co. creates a computer training program for its employees, some of whom subsequently leave Upstream Chemical Co. and apply for programmer jobs at Downstream Beverage Co., which needs programmers and, thanks to Upstream's training program, now can escape the costs of training them.

Since Pigou, economists have understood that total social welfare would be increased if private consumption and production decisions were modified to take externalities into account. Movements toward optimality as understood by Pareto had not included the existence of externalities that might distort resource allocation away from maximum economic efficiency. Pigou's solution, which he put forward around 1920, called for the imposition of *taxes* on activities that, through *negative* externalities, create either welfare losses for others in their consumption activities or cost increases for others in their production activities. The same logic calls for the payment of *subsidies* for activities that, through *positive* externalities, either increase the welfare of others or lower their production cost. For example, it is widely accepted that education is a critical component of a society's cultural, social, and intellectual infrastructure. All residents benefit from the education of responsible citizens and leaders, not to mention education's significant contribution to the private economic well-being of individual members of society. Thus, every resident has a stake in education. For the economist, the primary case for subsiding education rests on the belief that it conveys positive externalities benefiting society as a whole due to a combination of positive welfare gains and cost of production decreases. By the logic of externalities, polluters should face a tax based upon the estimated damage caused by their pollution, i.e., their negative externalities. It is important to note that the argument for taxation rests *not* on moralistic or philosophical ideas but solely on grounds of *economic efficiency*. Such taxation makes the market system work better, but to do so the tax must exactly equal the cost of the negative externality. Similarly, a subsidy might be paid to a landowner, for example, who takes his or her land out of production and makes it available as a park or nature preserve. Again, the subsidy in this case should equal the benefit of the positive externality.

The Importance of Income Distribution

A very important condition is attached to any Pareto-optimizing change: Pareto-efficient policies such as the ones just discussed are conditional on society's distribution of income. The current distribution of income together with the preferences of the individual members of society give rise to the willingness-to-pay for goods, including environmental protection. If the distribution of income were changed, people might express different preferences and a willingness-to-pay for a different mix of goods, including environmental protection. Insofar as a society relies on individual preferences and willingness-to-pay as the means of determining what goods to produce, society also accepts, at least implicitly, the justice of the current distribution of income.

The Legacy of Keynes

Ironically, the twentieth century's most influential economist, John Maynard Keynes, made virtually no contribution to the evolving theory on externalities or externality-offsetting taxes. Lord Keynes' landmark work, *The General Theory of Employment, Interest, and Money*, published in 1936 in the midst of the Great Depression, described a radically new macroeconomic approach that centered on creating an activist, interventionist government which, through aggressive monetary and fiscal policies and other economic controls, would smooth out the worst fluctuations of the business cycle. It is largely due to Keynesian policies in the period after World War II that the world's market economies experienced, depending on one's viewpoint, either an era of unprecedented economic growth or ruinous inflation and skyrocketing budget deficits.

Keynes' work exerted no direct influence over the development of environmental economics because it centered on macroeconomic theory and policies, while environmental economics is virtually all microeconomics. Nevertheless, the legacy of Keynes did influence the environmentalist movement in one very important way. To combat the Great Depression of the 1930s Keynesian economics advocated new forms and degrees of government control over the private sector beyond anything that had existed since the emergence of market-based economies. By justifying direct governmental intervention to fight the Depression, Keynesianism helped establish a social and political climate in favor of direct governmental intervention for other purposes as well. An unmistakable ancestral line of intellectual descent leads from the Keynesian interventions in the 1930s to the present day command-and-control interventions for environmental protection purposes.

Ecological Economics

There does exist an emerging alternative approach to microeconomics-based environmental economics that contains some macroeconomics discussion and analysis. This approach is coming to be known as ecological economics, although most of the work in the field is done by noneconomists. At this point, ecological economics is less a discipline and more a variated, multidisciplinary research program pursued by people from many different academic backgrounds with a common interest in ecological issues. While environmental economics maintains a positivist orientation grounded in the procedures of the scientific method, much of ecological economics is normatively oriented. One economist who has not avoided ecological economics but, on the contrary, is one of its founders is Herman Daly. Based at the World Bank, where he enjoyed an influential position for many years, Daly has argued that entire economies, like ordinary business firms, may have maximum desirable sizes.[8] This concept of an optimal scale for an entire economy, in turn, leads to issues of "sustainable development."

Sustainable Development

The idea of sustainable development originated with the Brundtland Report *Our Common Concern*, prepared for the World Commission on Environment and Development in 1987.[9] Sustainable development is commonly defined as development that meets the needs of the present without compromising the ability of future generations to meet their own needs. Some environmentalists see the idea as easily blending both economic prosperity today and preservation of the future environment; they see these two objectives as mutually supportive in the belief that we cannot have one without the other. But, it is just as easily argued that the two goals are competitive with each other because meeting environmental objectives "generally requires [the use of] resources that could otherwise be allocated for growth . . ., and vice versa."[10] In any case, the sustainable development idea is a very broad concept that does not seem to offer a scientifically operational problem. As we saw in Chapter Three, the first phase of the scientific method requires defining a problem so that it is susceptible to a deliberate, measurable, practical remedy.

Daly and other ecological economists also have questioned, on environmental grounds, the desirability of international free trade, which is a bedrock conclusion of mainstream economics. Many environmentalists who prefer command-and-control regulation dislike international free trade and the globalization of the marketplace because, as Krugman noted, "it epitomizes what they dislike about markets in general: the fact that nobody is in charge."[11] To most economists schooled in the tradition of mainstream economics, rejecting international free trade on environmental grounds amounts to "throwing the baby out with the bath water." It is a considerable concern to mainstream economists that the public, misguided into believing that international trade is the source of our economic problems — both environmental and nonenvironmental, like job losses — might turn protectionist, thereby undermining the tremendous amount of real economic benefit that globalization has provided for most people, both in this country and abroad.

Green Accounting

Daly has been sharply criticized by mainstream economists, who sometimes dismiss his work as "permeated with do-goodism and not enough hard science," rebukes that recently caused the MIT Press to reject his latest book even though it had commissioned the work.[12] But Daly is also at the forefront of another reform that many mainstream economists believe is long overdue. This reform is the introduction of so-called "Green Accounting." Daly views sustainable development as implying a consumption level that can be continued indefinitely without degrading capital stocks — not just man-made capital stocks, like buildings and equipment, but also "natural capital" stocks, like soil and atmospheric structure, forest, fish populations, and petroleum and mineral deposits. Therefore, sustainable development requires that nonrenewable "natural capital" stocks not be depleted any faster than the creation of renewable capital stocks, thereby holding steady the total stock of capital resources for the use by future generations.[13]

The problem here is knowing what these "natural capital" stocks are and, in particular, how current levels of production and consumption effect them. "Green Accounting" involves measuring *both* the benefits of current production and consumption activities *and* the environmentally damaging by-products from these production and consumption activities. An example Vice-President Al Gore gives in his book *Earth in the Balance* relates to a coal-fired power generating station that produces both kilo-watt-hours of electricity and tons of air polluting particulate.[14] It is necessary, *in the pursuit of economic rationality*, to measure and balance the benefit from electricity generation and the damages of the atmospheric emissions. Sulfur oxides from the power generating plant may cause, for example, crop losses, materials damage, visibility losses, and respiratory distress downwind from the power plant. The problem of *not counting* the environmental "bad" as well as the economic "good" from power generation received increased attention in 1996 when the EPA proposed new, tighter air quality standards for smog and soot. It is widely believed that much of the air pollution in New York, New Jersey, Connecticut, Rhode Island, and Massachusetts drifts in on the winds from other states, notably several states in the Midwest. Parts of the EPA's proposal to upgrade air quality standards received enthusiastic support from governors of Northeast states because they saw in these proposed new standards an opportunity to protect themselves from the consequences of power generation in Illinois, Michigan, Indiana, and Ohio.[15] The interstate political conflict that the proposed new standards created was considerable and the difficulties in measuring the environmental effects would be daunting. Nevertheless, from the viewpoint of economic rationality it is necessary that these damages be assessed and applied against the benefits of power generation. Moreover, the Principle of Compensation could play a useful role in solving the interstate conflict. Using cleaner-burning but more expensive fuels for power generation in the Midwest, all other things being equal, would increase the cost of electricity that residents of the Midwest states must pay while primarily benefiting residents of the Northeast states, who would suffer no corresponding increase in their electricity cost. The Principle of Compensation suggests that the Northeast states could compensate the Midwest states for converting to less-polluting fuels for power generation. This kind of compensation arrangement is precisely what Pareto had in mind over 100 years ago when he advocated movements toward a Pareto efficient allocation of resources, although he could not have envisioned the specific application to Midwest power generation. Nor could he have imagined the application of his idea to our earlier example of water allocations in California, which is the same type of economic-efficiency problem as wind-borne pollution from power generation in the Midwest.

As we shall see in Chapter Five, environmental damages inflicted on others are called "external costs" by economists and they play a central role in analyzing the optimal allocation of society's economic resources.

Notes

1. Eban S. Goodstein, *Economics and the Environment*, Englewood Cliffs, NJ, Prentice-Hall, 1995, 45-46.

2. Goodstein, 46.

3. Goodstein, 46.

4. Lester C. Thurow, *The Future of Capitalism : How Today's Economic Forces Shape Tomorrow's World*, New York, William Morrow, 1996, 260.

5. David W. Dunlap, "Community Interests Vs. Property Rights," *New York Times*, July 21, 1996, Sec 9, 1.

6. J.R. Clark an6161d J. Holton Wilson, *Survey of Economics*, Cincinnati, O., South-Western Publishing, 1997, 53.

7. John H. Cushman Jr., "U.S. Taking Cautious Approach in Talks on Global Warming," *New York Times*, December 8, 1996, International Edition, 14.

8. Herman E Daly, "Elements of Environmental Macroeconomics." See also Robert Costanza, Herman E. Daly, and Jay A. Bartholomew, "Goods, Agenda, and Policy Recommendations for Ecological Economics." Both essays are printed in *Ecological Economics: The Science and Management of Sustainability*, ed. by Robert Costanza, New York, Columbia University Press, 1991. Looking at the professional affiliations of the authors of the thirty-two articles in this remarkable collection of interdisciplinary papers, one sees immediately that relatively few of them reside professionally in traditional economics departments. Most have professional affiliations with environmental and ecological studies centers, energy and resource programs, and several with academic biology, chemistry and engineering departments.

9. World Commission on Environment and Development, *Our Common Future*, New York, Oxford University Press, 1987.

10. Faye Duchin and Glenn-Marie Lange, *The Future of the Environment: Ecological Economics and Technological Change*, New York, Oxford University Press, 1994, 5.

11. Paul Krugman, "We Are Not the World," *New York Times*, February 13, 1997, 33.

12. G. Pascal Zachary, "A 'Green Economist' Warns Growth May Be Overrated," *Wall Street Journal*, June 25, 1996, B-1.

13. Costanza, Daly, and Bartholomew, 8.

14. Al Gore, *Earth in the Balance: Ecology and the Human Spirit*, New York, Plume, 1992, 189-90.

15. John H. Cushman Jr., "Stricter Air Rules Could Place Focus on the Midwest," *New York Times*, December 1, 1996, 1.

Chapter 5
Economic Concepts and Environmental Goals

Opportunity Cost and Environmental Protection

Other than the multimillionaires among us, few people really would want to live in a pollution-free world, just as few people really would want to purchase the safest automobile that could be manufactured or eat the best food that could be flown in from Paris. In these cases, the underlying reason is always the same: the high cost of such undeniably attractive goods. Were our society to actually pursue a goal of zero pollution, for example, the real standard of living of most Americans would plummet. It is because goods other than pollution abatement — like food, clothing, housing, healthcare, art, music, recreation, and transportation — are also valuable to us that environmental goals cannot be treated as absolutes to be achieved regardless of cost.

The Concept of Opportunity Cost

Environmental protection and pollution abatement efforts already have made, and will continue to make, enormous demands on society's productive resources. Notwithstanding the fact that they are widely acknowledged and valuable social goals, it must always be borne in mind that the productive resources they require also could be used to satisfy other private or social goals. The overall scarcity of society's productive resources means that when resources are devoted to environmental protection, or any other goal, fewer resources are available for other purposes. Therefore, some opportunities must be foregone, which economists call opportunity cost. In general, the opportunity cost of using scarce productive resources to pursue any goal is the loss of the next most desired goal foregone in making that choice. Thus, an opportunity cost is really an opportunity lost.

Sometimes opportunity cost can be measured directly with money, as when you must forego seeing a movie with a $5 admission price because you spent your $5 on lunch. If you can afford both a $5 movie and a $5 lunch, then you must forego some other alternative, say, $5 worth of gasoline. Unless you have infinite money to spend, you must forego something when you spend $5 on lunch. Even for the richest people opportunity cost still exists. Although past and present billionaires like Bill Gates, Warren Buffett, George Soros, J.P. Morgan, John D. Rockefeller, and J. Paul Getty are (or were) wealthy enough to buy everything they might conceivably desire, they have limited time in which to enjoy their activities and acquisitions. Even billionaires cannot be in two different places at the same time, so even their choices imply opportunity costs. Like the rest of us, billionaires must choose among many competing uses for their scarce resources.

At a recent environmental seminar an environmental philosopher remarked that he really could not accept neoclassical economics because it holds that everything has a price and that just did not sit right with him. Of course it should not, because some of the most valuable things in life have no price, like the pleasures of enjoying a sunset or the companionship of a spouse or the company of one's children after a day of work. There are no prices attached to such activities, *but there certainly are costs*! The cost is the loss of the most valuable activity foregone, such as sleeping, studying, going out to dinner, or attending night school. The environmental philosopher had confused *price* with *cost*, a very common mistake.

Illustrations of Opportunity Cost

One illustration of the importance of the opportunity cost concept is provided by our command-and control approach to regulating health, safety, and environmental risks. Our present approach makes very little attempt to allocate scarce health, safety, and environmental protection resources where the actual threats of damage are greatest. In his highly regarded book on regulation, Stephen Breyer, then-Chief Judge of the United States

Court of Appeals for the First Circuit and now Justice of the United States Supreme Court, argued that misplaced public pressure and bureaucratic tunnel vision have badly skewed our regulatory priorities.[1] Frightened by inflammatory media reports, the public can become fixated on relatively minor risks that present small real dangers to life or health; an overly reactive Congress then pressures the regulators, who respond in turn by seeking to eliminate tiny risks, often with little or no scientific evidence documenting the supposed dangers. The result, Breyer concludes, is a random agenda and a patchwork of regulations and rules that lead to inconsistent regulatory results and economic absurdities in terms of opportunity cost.

One way to express the opportunity cost of such a random agenda is *a program's cost per life-year saved.* The results of a survey done by the Harvard University School of Public Health's Center for Risk Analysis provide some fascinating data on the effectiveness and cost of various health, safety, and environmental programs.[2] The Center's findings show that a life-year saved by preventing factories from releasing carcinogenic substances like formaldehyde and benzene generally costs more than $2.5 million. (The arithmetic can be a little tricky. The actual expense to save one life from death by cancer caused by formaldehyde and benzene might be, say, $50 million; but if the person lives an additional twenty years, the cost per life-year is $2.5 million: $50 million divided by twenty years equals $2.5 million per life-year.) Radiation controls have a cost of a year of life saved equal to $27.4 million. The most expensive intervention in the Center's study related to preventing releases of carcinogenic chloroform at pulp mills. This intervention cost an estimated $99.4 *billion* for each life-year saved. The chloroform controls at the 48 mills studied cost only $30.3 million annually, but it would be necessary to spend that much each year for more than 33,000 years to prevent a single fatal case of cancer due to carcinogenic chloroform at pulp mills. Dividing the annual cost by the tiny mortality risk yields the astronomical cost-to-benefit ratio for one life-year saved.[3]

While formaldehyde and benzene prevention programs at factories cost more than $2.5 million per life-year saved and radiation controls have a cost per life-year saved of $27.4 million, a year of life saved by a heart transplant costs only $104,000. The cost of a life-year saved by programs to avert cancer deaths is about $750,000, and the comparable figure for heart disease programs is a mere $14,000. Selective anticervical cancer screening programs for women over 60 save a life-year for each $11,000 expended. Water chlorination programs save a life-year for each $4,000, and flu shots save a life-year for each $600. According to the study, medical interventions generally save a life-year for less expenditure than injury-prevention measures, such as construction-safety rules or highway improvements, while injury-prevention interventions generally are cheaper per life-year saved than environmental regulations.

In opportunity cost terms, expensive environmental programs can, and often do, divert scarce funds from other interventions that are far more efficient at saving lives. Therefore, relatively ineffective environmental programs could be seen as *costing* lives instead of saving them. The cold-blooded nature of these economic comparisons doubtlessly offend some people and cause others to argue that more should be spent on all types of life-saving interventions. Nevertheless, given the limited resources now allocated to all such programs, the data clearly imply there are a large number of *lives not saved* because of inefficient interventions. It is estimated that if the $21.3 billion spent by the 185 major life-saving programs covered in the study were simply reallocated so that spending went only to the most effective interventions, *some 60,000 deaths in the U. S. alone could be averted annually at no additional total cost.* Too little environmental protection can obviously impair human health and reduce lifespans. But, it is also true that environmental goals and standards that are too high can skew society's scarce resources away from relatively more effective interventions, thereby unintentionally impairing human health and reducing lifespans, a dramatic example of the Law of Unintended Consequences. Another example of how good intentions can unintentionally cost lives relates to the "corporate average fuel economy" (CAFE) standards imposed on automobile manufacturers by the National Highway Traffic Safety Administration (NHTSA) to reduce air pollution from automobiles. In pursuing the one goal of reducing air pollution NHTSA officials ignore another danger that the agency's CAFE standards impose on automobile drivers and passengers. By forcing cars to become smaller and lighter — and therefore more dangerous — to meet air pollution reduction goals, CAFE is responsible for the deaths of thousands of people killed in traffic deaths every year.

Another perspective on opportunity cost relates to the new, tougher air pollution rules the Environment Protection Agency proposed in late 1996. These rules included more stringent limits and ground-level ozone, the main component of urban smog, and first-time limits on tiny airborne flecks of soot and ash, called fine particulates, which are emitted by diesel engines, power plants, and burning wood. The benefit from the tougher new rules, according to the EPA, would be an estimated 20,000 premature deaths averted each year, although the EPA does not say for how long the estimated deaths are postponed. Twenty thousand deaths postponed for however long is no small matter, but in a world of scarce economic resources some perspective on the EPA's number is necessary. More than 20,000 children in poor countries die *every 15 hours* (nearly 13 million deaths a year) from *preventable* malnutrition and disease. The hundreds of billions of dollars in new spending by producers, consumers, and governments in the U. S. required to implement the proposed new air pollution standards could also save many millions of lives in poor countries, were the economic resources allocated to that goal.

Similarly, at the Earth Summit in Rio de Janeiro in 1992 — which one environmentalist lauded as "a doorway" opening onto "more humane economics and benign technologies," "combined with greater concern for the vulnerability of Mother Earth and her creatures"[4] — the latest in environmental concerns, like global warming, PCBs, nuclear waste, and radon, were the focus of action. Western countries, including the U. S., agreed to devote tens of billions of dollars to help prevent global warming and the greenhouse effect, while ignoring the almost 8 million children who die each year in poor countries from drinking infected water and breathing befouled and deadly air.[5] (The exact 1993 figures are 3.8 million children under the age of five dead from preventable diarrhea diseases caused by impure water, according to UNICEF; and 4 million dead from preventable respiratory diseases caused primarily by air pollution, according to the World Health Organization.) At the present time, 1 1/3 billion people live in zones of "dangerously unsafe" air, at a time when air alerts at the "dangerous" level have became almost unknown in the West. Hundreds of millions of Chinese depend upon major rivers, like the Taizai River, that are now biologically dead, unable to support fish, while about 30 million Africans depend upon Lake Victoria, which is approaching biological death. Toxic chemicals in poor countries are close to uncontrolled, with direct discharge into sewers and rivers still the norm, a situation now nearly eliminated in developed countries like the U.S.[6] Unfortunately, mundane problems like toxic air in Calcutta and raw sewage in Uganda fail to capture the public's attention and emotions as do more exotic ecological threats, so they tend "to fall to the bottom of the agenda." Without a sense of priority or urgency among governmental leaders, they are chronically underfunded and crowded out in the competition for scarce economic resources.

Negative Externalities

When we drive a car to work or turn up the heat in our living room on a freezing winter evening, we generally do not take into account the effect of our actions in contributing to environmental problems. We usually think only about the private benefit to ourselves of getting to work or enjoying a warm home and the private cost of our gasoline or home heating bill. We do not ordinarily count, as an additional cost of our actions, an increase in the incidence of lung disease; forest and other physical property destruction; road congestion; smog creation; acid rain; or depletion of non-renewable natural resources, all of which can result, directly or indirectly, from our driving to work or heating our house. Such harmful side-effects of private activities are called negative externalities. *Negative externalities arise whenever one person's act of producing or consuming a good inflicts involuntary costs on others.*

Negative externalities occur when consumers and producers dump their unwanted wastes into the air, a water source, or onto public land. These unwanted wastes are commonly called pollutants, and the act of dumping them is polluting. The dumping may be intentional or unintentional, calculated or innocent, but the negative environmental effects are the same. We are all a direct source of pollution whenever we drive a car that emits exhaust fumes: the primary ingredient of smog is ground-level ozone, which is formed in the atmosphere when hydrocarbons from gasoline vapors, solvents, and other pollutants combine in daylight with nitrogen oxide emissions from cars as well as industrial facilities. The huge potential for air pollution from private automobiles can be grasped from the fact that U.S. cars and trucks burn 219,000 gallons of gasoline *every minute* of *every day* of the year. In addition, we are sources of pollution whenever we use electricity for light, heat, and air conditioning: power generating plants that burn oil help create ozone, while coal-burning power plants emit sulfur dioxide, which can travel long distances in the upper air and cause "acid raid" on unsuspecting residents of distant states and even foreign countries. The companies that manufacture our consumer products may use local rivers, lakes, or harbors as dumping grounds for their unwanted wastes. Or, they may contain their unwanted wastes on private land, but once the wastes are dumped they may penetrate the soil and move sideways. Pollution of groundwater supplies by gasoline and other petroleum products can be caused by leakages from, say, the underground storage tanks at our friendly neighborhood service station. One oil industry expert has estimated that one-third of the nation's one million-plus service station underground storage tanks may be leaking today. Drinking water polluted by gasoline can cause anemia, kidney disease, nervous system disorder, and cancer.

The Problem of Market Failure

Thinking about environmental threats in impersonal terms like negative externalities suggests that pollution usually does not originate with intrinsically defective or dangerous people. There are many defective and dangerous situations, however, that can lead to polluting behavior. For economists, pollution is not the result of bad character or modern technology or the laws of nature, but of a flaw in our market system. The flaw exists because *free market prices of productive resources and the goods they produce are efficient guides for resource allocation only when property rights are well defined and easily enforceable. Pollution and other damaging environmental effects occur because open-access common-property resources like air, water, and public land have no well-defined, enforceable private ownership rights over them.* Many environmentalists believe, like Aldo Leopold in his *Sand County Almanac*, that we abuse the environment "because we regard it as a commodity belonging to us." Most environmental economists believe the opposite: we abuse the environment because we regard it as a commodity belonging to no one, or at least not to us. Simply put, when people own rights to private resources, they have an abiding interest in seeing those resources protected and used efficiently. But when no one in particular owns the rights to common-property resources, no one in particular has an abiding interest in seeing those resources protected and efficiently used.

The Tragedy of the Commons

Most examples of pollution occur in connection with *open-access common-property resources*. Underground water, surface lakes and waterways, harbors, the oceans, public spaces like parks, gardens, and national forests, even the atmosphere itself are all common-property resources. The specification and enforcement of private property rights in these cases either do not exist or are impractical because individual private owners would find it prohibitively expensive to exclude others from using the property or to charge for its use. Thus, open-access common-property resources tend to be treated by consumers and producers as *if they were free resources*. Since there is no charge for their use, consumers and producers have no direct incentive to protect them or to economize on their use. For the economist, the basic problem here is the lack of proper incentives rather than deficient moral character. The wrong economic signals are sent by our market system that put a zero price on using some of our most valuable resources. Economists use the term *market failure to describe a situation in which incorrect price signals are sent to consumers and producers*. This failure of markets to correctly price valuable resources results in their being undercared for, underprotected, and grossly overused, a situation Garrett Hardin poetically described as "the Tragedy of the Commons." While the "Tragedy" is horrific in its consequences for the natural environment, to the economist its ultimate cause is not difficult to understand.

The problems associated with open-access common-property resources are not limited to consumers and producers converting them into waste disposal facilities. The problems also include overusing our common-property resources as harvest grounds for commercial clamming, shrimping, oystering, lobstering, and fishing. From 1970 to 1990, the world's commercial fishing fleet more than doubled, with the result that by 1994 some of the once abundant fish and oyster species verged on commercial extinction. Although environmental degradation of the oceans played a small role in the decline of marine life, according to a Worldwatch Institute report the primary cause of dwindling fish and shellfish populations has been overfishing, that is, the overuse of open-access common-property resources. Government policies, Worldwatch noted, have deliberately promoted and subsidized the expansion of the large-scale fishing industry, which has greatly accelerated the overharvesting.

Environmental problems also involve overusing open-access common-property resources for recreational purposes, like boating on rivers and lakes, as well as hunting, fishing, and camping in wilderness areas. An example of the common-pool problem leading to recreational overuse is now occurring at Otsego Lake, one of New York State's most beautiful and historically important bodies of water. It was at this lake 200 years ago that James Fenimore Cooper formed his ideas about the wilderness: Ostego Lake is in fact the Glimmerglass of his masterpiece of early American fiction, *Leatherstocking Tales*, which presents one of the earliest views of nature not as a threatening force to be conquered but as something fragile to be preserved. Just as Cooper showed in *Leatherstocking Tales* how people are capable of degrading their own environment to their own detriment, his beloved Otsego Lake is now in dire condition. Serious damage has already been done to its plant and animal biodiversity and over the last decade the lake has lost two-thirds of its area where cold-water fish can survive. The damage stems from motorboat engines, which pollute the water with hydrocarbons and stir mud and nutrients from the bottom and shoreline. The nutrients consume vast quantities of oxygen, destroying the environment where cold-water fish live. Motorboats are now launched onto the lake at several public and private sites. A huge new motorboat ramp, complete with a parking lot for cars and trailers, is now scheduled to be built at Glimmerglass State Park, near the lake's northern end. The three likeliest ramp sites are located in wetlands, many acres of which would have to be filled in for roads and parking. The plan also calls for dredging and building a pier at least 50 feet wide and 150 feet long. The New York State Department of Environmental Conservation and the Office of Parks, Recreation, and Historic Preservation have been active regarding the plan for a new ramp, but not in the way one might think. Far from opposing the scheme, the Department of Environmental Conservation and the Office of Parks are the chief sponsors of it, planning to spend at least $500,000 to $1 million on the project, not to mention the millions of dollars later on to repair future ecological damage that will surely result from the use of many more high-speed motorboats on the lake.[7] This story illustrates not a tale of big business cruelly manipulating a compliant state government to get its way on pollution, but a state government responding to public pressures from ordinary citizens for goods that are commonly provided and subsidized by government, at the inevitable opportunity cost of fewer educational, health care, and other governmental services available for the non-motorboating public in New York.

Measuring Market Distortion

For most noneconomists, the idea of overusing an open-access common-property resource simply conveys the general notion that a resource is "used a lot," perhaps to the point of "ruining" it or "running out of it." For economists, however, overusing a resource has a specific *analytical* meaning. Imagine that consumers and producers could no longer use open-access common-property resources for free. Instead, imagine that they were required to pay a tax for their use of a common-property resource. As a result of the tax, the final price consumers paid for, say, a gallon of gasoline or a pound of fish would now reflect *the true full* cost of consuming gasoline *and* dirtying the air, or of enjoying a fish dinner *and* depleting the fish population. The power generating company would have to pay for using the air for dumping, and such costs normally would be passed along by the company to consumers; the price consumers paid for electricity would now reflect the damage others suffer due to polluted air. In all these cases, consumers would pay a higher price, one that would more closely correspond to the full cost of what is produced and consumed. The new price would depend on the amount of the tax. This idea is what economists call "internalizing an externality," that is, changing *private costs* so that they reflect the *full costs to society* of a private activity.

Because the final price paid for gasoline or electricity would be higher by the amount of the tax, smaller quantities of these goods would be purchased. (As we shall see in Chapter Six, an inverse relationship exists between the price paid for a good by consumers and the quantity of the good consumers will buy.) Because smaller quantities of gasoline and electricity would be bought, pollution would decline. How much pollution declines would depend on the size of the gasoline and electricity price increases. The regulatory authority would determine the size of the price increases when it determines the size of the taxes. In the example of overfishing, the harvesting of the oceans would decrease because fewer fish would be demanded by consumers due to higher fish prices.

The degree of market failure is measured by the amount of overconsumption caused by under-pricing a good. Market failure is measured by *the difference between* (1) the quantity consumed when people pay a low price that reflects only a part of the full cost of producing and consuming the good, less (2) the quantity consumed when people pay a higher price that reflects the full cost of producing and consuming the good. *The extra pollution due to overconsumption measures the overuse of open-access common-property resources*. An example of these calculations is shown in Table 5-1.

In summary, free markets suffer market failure when producers and consumers are not charged for their use of open-access common-property resources. When this occurs, free market prices fail to convey the full costs to society of producing and consuming goods. The economist's solu-

TABLE 5-1. Calculating Market Distortion and Environmental Overuse

Price of Good X	Amount of Consumed Good X	Description	Amount of Resulting Pollution
$1.00	60	Larger quantity of Good X consumed when consumer pays a low price that covers only partial cost of producing and consuming Good X, Less:	30 units
$2.25	20	Smaller quantity of Good X consumed when consumer pays a higher price that covers full cost of producing and consuming Good X.	10 units
	40	Amount of overconsumption of Good X, i.e., the market distortion caused by underpricing Good X. Amount of overuse of environment, i.e., the extra pollution caused by the overconsumption of Good X.	20 units

tion to the market failure problem is to correct for the underpricing of a good by imposing an additional charge, sometimes called a pollution tax. As we shall see in future chapters, a system of environmental protection involving pollution charges combined with tradable pollution permits achieves remarkable efficiency advantages in comparison with a command-and-control approach to environmental regulation.

Notes

1. Stephen Breyer, *Breaking the Vicious Circle: Toward Effective Risk Regulation*, Cambridge, Mass., Harvard University Press, 1993, 8.

2. David Stipp, "Prevention May be Costlier Than a Cure," *Wall Street Journal*, July 6, 1994, B-1.

3. By way of providing some perspective on the magnitude of these numbers, several studies show "that labor unions, when free to bargain about safety rules, will insist upon rules that value statistical lives saved at around $5-6 million." See Breyer, 22, and his sources, 97, footnote #110.

4. Philip Shabecoff, *A New Name For Peace: International Environmentalism, Sustainable Development, and Democracy*, Hanover, N.H., University Press of New England, 1996, as quoted by Mark Dowie, "Green Giant," *New York Times Book Review*, June 9, 1996, 37.

5. Gregg Easterbrook, "Forget PCB's, Radon, Alar," *New York Times Sunday Magazine*, September 11, 1994, 60-4.

6. Gregg Easterbrook, *A Moment On The Earth: The Coming Age of Environmental Optimism*, New York, Penguin Books, 1995, 578-9.

7. Henry S.F. Cooper, Jr., "Motorboats on Glimmerglass?!," *New York Times*, September 16, 1995, Sec. L, 19.

Chapter 6
Analyzing Market Failure

Economic rationality suggests that the best policy for accomplishing efficient environmental protection is *not* to abandon an otherwise remarkably efficient market system. The current command-and-control environmental regulatory approach, however, comes very near to doing exactly this, often creating the same kinds of gross economic inefficiencies that characterized precapitalist mercantilism in Europe and centralized economic planning in the former Soviet Union and Eastern Bloc economies. Pollution reduction can be achieved at lower cost by using the strengths of the market system, but with the incentives of the market system altered to correct for the existence of negative externalities. To alter market incentives, the market prices of goods produced and consumed must be raised (or lowered) when negative (or positive) externalities exist, since the effects of externalities in production and consumption are not reflected in the goods' free market prices. For example, the market price of gasoline would be raised to reflect the negative externalities that burning gasoline imposes on society at large.

In this chapter, the negative externalities that arise with open-access common-property resources will be analyzed, showing how market failure occurs, its effects, and the use of a pollution tax to correct for these effects.

Total Private Benefit

Private benefit (called "utility" in economist's jargon) refers to the satisfaction a person receives when privately consuming a good. The reasons for an individual's consumption of, say, gasoline might be driving for pleasure or to work, shopping, visiting a sick aunt, or attending school. Whatever the reasons, total private benefit depends on the person's level of consumption — a higher consumption level giving more total private benefit.

Take the example of a hypothetical consumer living in, say, the New York-New Jersey-Connecticut metropolitan area (hereafter, NNC). Suppose that the total private benefit this consumer receives each month from consuming gasoline is depicted by the curve TBp in Figure 1. If the individual consumes no gasoline, there is no benefit from gasoline that month. As the amount of gasoline consumed in a month increases, the person's total benefit increases, so if 50 gallons are consumed he/she receives 1750 units of benefit. The cardinal numbers used to illustrate the individual's total private benefit are hypothetical, but *the pattern* of how total private benefit changes with the amount of gasoline consumed is very special.

Marginal Private Benefit

In Figure 1 the pattern of how total private benefit changes with the amount of gasoline consumed is determined by the famous Law of Diminishing Marginal Benefit (or Diminishing Marginal Utility in economists' jargon). Figure 1 shows that the individual receives a continuously decreasing *marginal* private benefit from consuming more and more gasoline. (Marginal simply means *the amount added* due to *the last unit* of change.) The *marginal* private benefit is the amount added to the individual's *total* private benefit from, say, the last 10-gallons of gasoline consumed in the month. A close look at Figure 1 will show that when consumption of gasoline per month increases from 0 to 10, *total* private benefit from gasoline increases from 0 to 500. Thus, the *marginal* private benefit of the first 10 gallons consumed is 500 units. When consumption increases from 10 to 20 gallons, total private benefit increases from 500 to 880, so the marginal private benefit of the second 10 gallons consumed is only 330 units. As the individual consumes more and more gasoline, the marginal benefit he/she receives from gasoline continually decreases. A pattern of continuous decreases in marginal benefit as consumption increases reflects the Law of Diminishing Marginal Benefit.

The MBp curve in Figure 2 depicts the declining *marginal* private benefit of each 10-gallon increment in the individual's gasoline consumption during the month. The declining MBp curve is shown passing through

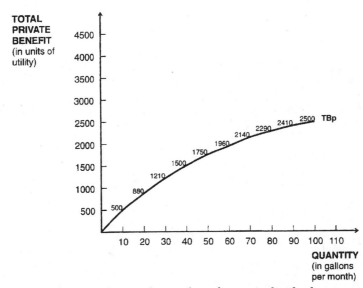

FIG. 1. The TBp curve shows that, for an individual consumer, the total private benefit from consuming gasoline (measured on the vertical axis) rises at a decreasing rate as the quantity of gasoline consumed per month (measured on the horizontal axis) increases.

a declining series of bars. It is shown this way because it is *the change in gasoline consumption*, from 0 to 10 gallons or 10 to 20 gallons, that produces the *marginal* benefit of 500 or 380. In Figure 2, the marginal private benefit is positive but diminishes continuously because each successive 10 gallon increase in gasoline consumed per month adds less and less to the individual's total private benefit. The individual's marginal private benefit from consuming more and more gasoline declines because for a rational person the most important purposes for driving are taken care of first, before less urgent needs are met. Also, note that the individual's total private benefit curve TBp in Figure 1 is increasing at a decreasing rate; mathematically, the falling marginal private benefit curve MBp in Figure 2 is the same as the decreasing slope of the TBp curve in Figure 1.

Individual Demand

An individual's demand for gasoline is based on the marginal private benefit the individual receives from consuming gasoline, as shown by the Di=MBp curve in Figure 3. The demand curve Di depicts the different quantities of gasoline the individual would be willing to consume at vari-

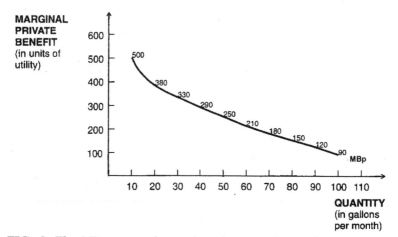

FIG. 2. The MBp curve shows that, for an individual consumer, the marginal private benefit from consuming gasoline (measured on the vertical axis) continuously decreases as the quantity of gasoline consumed per month (measured on the horizontal axis) increases.

ous gasoline prices. For simplicity, we assume that only one gasoline price exists in NCC for the time period in question, so only one of these different quantities of gasoline actually will be purchased by the individual. The important point is that the demand curve expresses an individual's willingness to buy different quantities of gasoline at various prices. The downward slope of the demand curve means that an inverse relationship exists between the price of gasoline and the quantity of gasoline the individual consumes per month, which is known as the *Law of Demand*. The downward slope of the individual's demand curve is consistent with the diminishing marginal private benefit the consumer receives from more and more gasoline consumption. Diminishing marginal private benefit from gasoline consumption means that each successive increase in gallons consumed is subjectively valued less and less by the individual, while the negative slope of the demand curve reflects the fact that the individual is willing to pay less and less for more and more gallons purchased. (Technically, the demand curve's negative slope is caused by what economists call the substitution and income effects in consumption, but these effects need not be discussed here.)

Of course, the individual's willingness to buy gasoline is effected by many other determinants besides the price of gasoline. Some of the other determinants of gasoline demand are the individual's tastes and prefer-

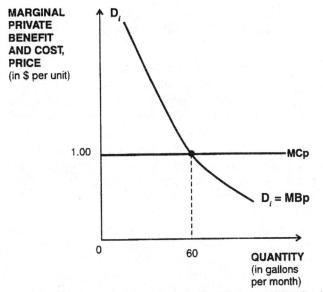

FIG. 3. The Di = MBp curve shows that, for an individual consumer, the marginal private benefit from consuming gasoline — and the price the consumer would be willing to pay for gasoline (measured on the vertical axis) — continuously decreases as the amount of gasoline consumed per month (measured on the horizontal axis) increases. The MCp curve shows a given market price the individual must pay per gallon of gasoline demanded ($1.00 per gallon).

---

ences; the individual's income; the prices of goods that are substitutes for consuming gasoline, like bus, taxi, or subway fares; and the prices of goods complementary to consuming gasoline, like car insurance, tires, and tolls. For a given demand curve, all these other determinants are assumed to be constant. This reflects the economist's use of the "ceterus paribus" assumption, meaning "all other things being constant." If any of the determinants other than the price of gasoline were to change, the result would be called *a change in demand*, and consequently the entire demand curve in Figure 3 would shift rightward (called a demand increase) or leftward (a demand decrease). On the other hand, if the amount of gasoline consumed were to change because of a change in the price of gasoline, the result would be called *a change in the quantity demanded*. This is the conventional language in economic analysis to keep separate the different types of factors that can effect an individual's consumption demand.

Private Cost, External Cost, and Social Cost

The horizontal curve MCp in Figure 3 shows the marginal private cost of a gallon of gasoline consumed by the individual. Since the individual is only one of millions of gasoline consumers in NNC, the effect of changes in his/her demand on gasoline prices is negligible. Consequently, the individual can buy all the gasoline he/she wants at the prevailing market price, say, $1.00/gallon; the horizontal MCp curve in Figure 3 depicts this constant price. The individual bases his/her consumption decision on the marginal private cost of buying gasoline. Given the price ($1.00/gallon), together with the individual's demand for gasoline, the equilibrium quantity of gasoline purchased is 60 gallons per month. At $1.00 per gallon, the marginal private cost (MCp) of a gallon of gasoline to the individual equals the marginal private benefit (MBp) to the individual from consuming a gallon of gasoline.

As we have seen, however, negative externalities occur with the consumption of gasoline. The fact that fossil fuels are burned helps create smog and air pollution, not to mention the effects on road congestion from driving private cars. These external side effects impose pollution and congestion costs on society as a whole. In a full cost sense, the private act of driving and consuming gasoline involves not only the individual's private cost of gasoline but also the external costs associated with smog, air pollution, and traffic congestion *for which the individual is not charged with a free market price of $1.00/gallon*. In other words, the free market price fails to reflect the cost to society that is imposed by the negative externalities created by consuming gasoline.

Costs to society caused by negative externalities are called external costs. Market failure occurs when a free market price excludes any charge for external costs. Assume that the marginal external cost imposed on society by air pollution and traffic congestion is, say, equivalent to $1.25 per gallon of gasoline. The marginal external cost associated with one gallon of gasoline is shown in Figure 4 by the vertical distance between the marginal private cost curve MCp and the marginal social cost curve MCs, i.e., the distance x-y. *Marginal social cost, or full cost, is defined as the sum of the marginal private cost plus the marginal external cost* imposed on society. At a consumption level of, say, 60 gallons per

Marginal Private Cost
+ <u>Marginal External Cost</u>
Marginal Social Cost (= Full Cost)

month, marginal social cost (distance w-y) is greater than the individual's marginal private benefit from the last unit of gasoline consumed (distance w-x). In other words, the full cost of the individual's consumption of the

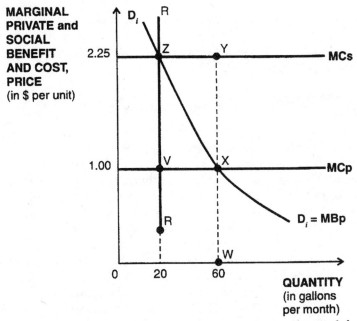

FIG. 4. The Di = MBp and MCp curves are unchanged from Figure 3. The MCs curve depicts a higher market price the individual must pay per gallon of gasoline after the addition of a "pollution tax" of $1.25 per gallon. The pollution tax reflects the marginal external cost imposed on society by the consumption of an additional gallon of gasoline.

last gallons of gasoline is $2.25, but this gasoline consumption has a marginal private benefit to the individual of only $1.00. Because the marginal social cost exceeds the marginal private benefit at 60 gallons per month, this level of gasoline consumption *indicates a failure of the market. Too much gasoline is produced and consumed due to the underpricing of gasoline.*

Correcting for Market Failure

For society as a whole, the efficient level of gasoline consumption occurs where the value to the individual of the last unit of gasoline consumed just equals the full cost of the last unit of gasoline consumed. This equality is found where the individual's demand, or marginal private benefit, curve Di=MBp intersects the marginal social cost curve MCs, shown as point z in Figure 4. The point of equality where Di= MCs implies that, from a social welfare viewpoint, as opposed to the viewpoint of the individual's purely private welfare, a decrease in the individual's monthly gasoline consumption to 20 gallons per month is indicated. As a practical matter, how could such a reduction in the individual's gasoline consumption be accomplished?

Consumer Rationing

One seemingly straightforward method for reducing the individual's gasoline consumption would be a system of gasoline rationing. Philosophically, consumption rationing dovetails nicely with the command-and-control approach to regulation. The higher authorities simply allocate everyone, say, 20 gallons of gasoline a month. Such allocations were actually made during World War II, although not for environmental reasons. But a consumer rationing system is not nearly as simple as it appears at first glance. Presumably, the government wishes to treat each individual fairly, or equitably. But *equitable* treatment is *not* the same as *equal* treatment. For example, if you live twenty miles from work and I live five miles from my job, equity considerations should require that you receive a larger gasoline ration than I receive. Or, if you are a salesperson whose work keeps you on the road three days a week while my job does not require me to be on the road at all, again on equity grounds you should receive a larger gasoline ration than I should receive. Equity requires *equal treatment of people in equal circumstances and unequal treatment of people in unequal circumstances*. Thus, establishing equity in rationing would require the regulatory authorities to know and evaluate the gasoline needs of every individual in the country in order to ration the correct amount of gasoline to each person. In reality, the government has no realistic way of knowing and evaluating the gasoline needs of 260,000,000 individuals. As a result, it has no practical choice except to ignore equity in favor of *simple equality*, say, 20 gallons a month to everyone. But such a one-size-fits-all gasoline allocation is also unworkable because, for example, traveling salespersons could not function and workers who live twenty miles from work would have to quit their jobs. Equal treatment would be grossly generous to persons living in New York City but impossibly inadequate for people living in rural areas without access to mass transit. *At bottom, simple equality in rationing is both unfair and economically inefficient because it does not recognize and respond to the differing needs of people for gasoline*. No rationing scheme can, in practice, direct gasoline to where it is most needed and valued as a price system does automatically. To be workable at all, rationing boards must be established across the country to hear and adjudicate countless requests for more gasoline. During World

War II, when consumption rationing of many goods was a fact of life, tens of thousands of government bureaucrats were employed for the sole purpose of listening to citizen appeals and administering dozens of rationing schemes.

Even though consumption rationing is unfair, economically inefficient, and very costly to administer, the idea has one *apparent* advantage. At first glance, it seems like the individual's gasoline consumption can be held to 20 gallons per month while also keeping the gasoline price from rising above $1.00 per gallon. Under a rationing system, the rationed supply of gasoline to the individual is fixed at 20 gallons per month, or curve RR in Figure 4. However, by referring to the demand curve DD we know that at a price of $1.00 per gallon *the individual's true demand is for 60 gallons per month.* This means that for the individual a "shortage" of 40 gallons per month exists. A "shortage" is defined as an excess of quantity demanded (60 gallons) over the quantity supplied (20 gallons) at a given price ($1.00/gallon). The inescapable problem with every rationing system is that at any regulated price below the equilibrium price (in our example, $2.25), individuals want to purchase more than the rationed amount. In practice, it is often next-to-impossible for the government to design systems that are sufficiently sophisticated in their controls and harsh enough in their penalties to prevent them from doing so.

The inevitable consequence of shortages caused by rationing is the development of black-markets. Black-markets include many types of illegal activities and devices, such as sellers withholding supplies from regulated markets so as to sell them under-the-counter in free markets at higher prices; buyers bribing officials in charge of assigning ration allocations; and simply purchasing other people's ration stamps. All of these activities were common in the U. S. during World War II. They were the ordinary way of life in the former Soviet Union and Eastern Bloc countries under their command-and-control economies and they remain typical in Cuba and mainland China. For any rationing scheme to be truly effective over the long run, government must resort to a level of authoritarianism — enforced by tens of thousands of checkers, investigators, auditors, and drastic enforcement penalties — that is inconsistent with the personal freedoms associated with Western liberal values.

A Consumption-Based Pollution Tax

The only other feasible approach to the problem of reducing gasoline consumption is by taxing gasoline purchases. The size of the tax should *not* be determined by non-environmental considerations, like raising revenue to reduce the federal government budget deficit, which was the Clinton administration's rationale in 1993 when it proposed a misguided BTU energy tax plan. *The appropriate gasoline tax is one that equalizes the marginal private benefit from consuming gasoline with the marginal social cost of consuming gasoline.* A tax on each gallon equal to the marginal external cost of gasoline consumption accomplishes this equality. A pollution tax equal to x-y in Figure 4 raises the individual's marginal private cost of gasoline consumption to equal the marginal social cost of gasoline consumption. The economist would say that the individual's negative externalities have been internalized. With the pollution tax of x-y, the MCs curve becomes the relevant marginal cost curve to the individual in making a consumption decision. The quantity of gasoline demanded by the individual decreases to 20 gallons a month because at 20 gallons the consumer equates the marginal private benefit from consuming gasoline to the marginal social cost of consuming gasoline.

The new price of $2.25/gallon and the corresponding reduction in demand to 20 gallons per month represents a socially efficient, or optimal, allocation of resources. An efficient allocation of resources means that net social benefit is maximized. As shown in Figure 4, net social benefit cannot be increased by the individual consuming either more or less gasoline: with gasoline consumption above 20 gallons per month, marginal social cost exceeds marginal private benefit, so net social benefit would increase with less consumption; and with consumption below 20 gallons per month, marginal private benefit exceeds marginal social cost, so net social benefit would increase with more consumption.

The net social gain that results from reducing the individual's gasoline consumption to its socially efficient level is shown by the triangle x-y-z in Figure 4. The same triangle measures the net social cost of the negative externalities caused by the individual's consumption without the pollution tax; in other words, the triangle x-y-z reflects the amount by which the total social cost exceeds the total private benefit with consumption at 60 gallons per month. Although gasoline consumption is reduced at a price of $2.25/gallon, pollution is not altogether eliminated at point z, since the private driving of automobiles still occurs. However, with the higher price of gasoline it is to be expected that consumers would shift toward fuel-sipping cars and away from hulking sport utility vehicles and light trucks, which millions of Americans now prefer due to the lowest gasoline prices in the industrialized world. There would be other attempts to cope as well, such as cutting back on less essential driving, more car pooling, and flex-time at work. Also, other transportation alternatives, like buses, subways, and bicycles, become more attractive and more competitive for the consumer's income. Finally — and less happily — with higher gasoline prices there would be an increase in income inequality. In general, the *proportion* of consumer income spent on gasoline (as well as other forms of energy) decreases as consumer income increases, although the absolute amount of income spent on gasoline (and other forms of energy) increases. This fact means that a gasoline tax has a *regressive* effect on income distribution. With a regressive tax, the percentage of income paid in taxes falls as income increases. Nevertheless, at point z the individual's private consumption of gasoline no longer generates a total marginal private and external cost in excess of marginal private benefit, such as occurs at point x.

Market Demand

The analysis of the socially efficient amount of gasoline consumption by the individual easily extends to the socially efficient amount of gasoline consumption for all consumers taken together. If the demands by every individual gasoline consumer in the NNC area are added together by means of a horizontal summation of each individual demand curve, a demand curve for gasoline *in the market as a whole* results. In graphing the market demand curve, the vertical axis would be unchanged from Figures 3 and 4, but the horizontal axis now would measure gasoline consumption per month in terms of, say, 100 million gallon units per month instead of 10 gallon units.

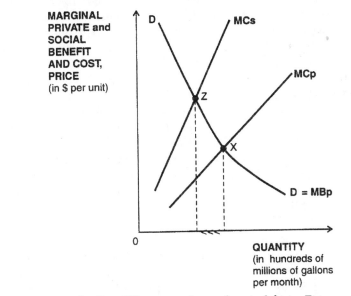

FIG. 5. The D = MBp curve is unchanged from Figures 3 and 4. The MCp shows that, for the market as a whole, consumers must pay an increasing price per gallon of gasoline (measured on the vertical axis) as the number of gallons of gasoline consumed per month (measured on the horizontal axis) increases. The MCs curve equals the sum of the MCp curve plus the marginal external cost imposed on society by the private consumption of gasoline.

As shown in Figure 5, the marginal private cost curve for gasoline in the market as a whole slopes upward-to-the-right. The positive slope of the marginal private cost curve in the market as a whole is easily explained. Changes in *individual* gasoline purchases are minuscule in their effects on production cost and so these effects can be ignored, but changes in the market demand for gasoline are large, in the magnitude of hundreds of millions of gallons. Large changes in gasoline purchases would definitely cause changes in production cost. The higher per unit cost of producing larger quantities of gasoline causes the marginal private cost curve (MCp) in the market as a whole to slope upward-to-the-right.

The marginal external cost associated with gasoline consumption for the market as a whole is added to the marginal private cost curve for gasoline to arrive at the marginal social cost of gasoline consumption. The result is an upward-sloping curve that shows a rising marginal social cost of gasoline consumption, MCs, and lies above the MCp curve by the amount of external costs. That is, the MCs curve is the sum of the MCp plus the marginal external cost imposed on society by the consumption of gasoline. A pollution tax is appropriate to correct for the marginal external cost of private gasoline consumption. The tax will cause consumers to reduce the quantity of gasoline consumed to the point where the marginal private benefit equals the marginal social cost of gasoline consumption. The upward-sloping MCs curve intersects with the downward-sloping market demand curve MBp at point z. This intersection determines the socially efficient amount of gasoline consumption. Gasoline consumption is considerably less than if consumers simply balanced marginal private benefit against marginal private cost (point x). The concept of a socially efficient, or optimal, allocation of society's resources is a valuable extension of environmentalist thinking because it specifically takes into account the *private* benefit that individuals receive through private consumption activities (like driving) as well as the *social* benefit that individuals receive (like enjoying cleaner air and less road congestion).

A Production-Based Pollution Tax

In the same way consumers create negative externalities when driving cars, producers can create negative externalities in their production processes. Indeed, one way almost everyone contributes to pollution is through purchasing goods that are produced in ways that pollute open-access common-property resources. In this section, we illustrate and extend the logic of negative externalities to the behavior of producers.

Suppose that the market demand for electricity in the NNC area is represented by D=MBp in Figure 6. The curve reflects consumers' marginal private benefit from electricity consumption in the market as a whole. For the moment, assume the marginal private unit cost of generating electricity is constant, shown by the horizontal curve MCp. Also, assume that

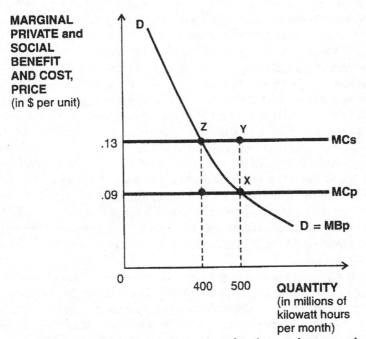

FIG. 6. The D = MBp curve shows that, for the market as a whole, the marginal private benefit from consuming electricity — and the price consumers would be willing to pay for electricity (measured on the vertical axis) — *continuously decreases* as the amount of electricity consumed per month (measured on the horizontal axis) increases. The MCp curve shows a given market price consumers must pay per kilowatt (9 cents per kilowatt). The MCs curve equals the sum of the MCp curve plus the marginal external cost imposed on society by the private production and consumption of electricity.

a fixed technological relationship exists between generating electricity and the creation of negative externalities like air pollution, as shown by the distance x-y. (The assumptions of a constant marginal private unit cost of generating electricity and a fixed relationship between electricity generation and pollution creation are simplifications that are dropped later.) Without a tax, purely private cost-benefit calculations result in a level of electricity consumption of 500 million kilowatt hours per month, shown at point x where MBp = MCp. At point x, the marginal private benefit of the last kilowatt hour purchased equals $0.09 and the marginal private cost of purchasing that kilowatt hour is also $0.09. *But when the marginal external cost of air pollution from electricity generation is included, the marginal cost of a kilowatt hour rises to $0.13.* Therefore, a pollution tax is called for: a tax equal to $0.04 would internalize the negative externalities associated with generating and consuming electricity.

The effect of a $0.04 unit tax on electricity consumption would be a reduction in the quantity of electricity generated and consumed from 500 million kilowatt hours per month to 400 million hours, shown at point z. Note carefully that although power companies are now generating the socially efficient, or optimal, amount of electricity, air pollution is not eliminated. To the economist, social efficiency means a level of electricity generation and consumption that maximizes net social benefit. In this case, net social benefit would diminish if either fewer than 400 million kilowatt hours *or* more than 400 million kilowatt hours were produced and consumed per month. It follows that the resulting amount of air pollution abatement at 400 million kilowatt hours *is society's optimal amount of pollution abatement.* Alternatively, we could say that the amount of air pollution remaining with 400 million kilowatt hours is *society's optimal level of air pollution.*

From a purely economic perspective, the most efficient means of achieving society's optimal amount of pollution abatement is a unit tax on electricity consumption sufficient to reduce pollution to the appropriate level. However, as Anderson points out in his study of four European countries (Denmark, France, Germany, and the Netherlands), this solution might require politically unacceptably high tax rates. As a second best alternative, he argues that lower tax rates *when combined with subsidies for pollution abatement* can provide the needed incentives for investment in pollution control technology. Polluting industries in his four countries have been the frequent recipients of substantial subsidies for pollution control equipment, financed by funds that have been previously collected in fees from the polluting industries themselves.[1]

Notes

1. Mickael Skou Anderson, *Governance by Green Taxes: Making Pollution Prevention Pay*, Manchester, U.K., Manchester University Press, 1994.

Chapter 7
Environmental Protection
as an Economic Good

Socially Efficient Pollution Abatement

Environmental protection and pollution abatement are economic goods because the use of scarce productive resources is required to achieve them. Of all the principles economics has to offer, the most important is that every economic good has a cost, although that cost may not be stated explicity in terms of money. No economically rational individual would purchase a good without considering both its cost and its benefit. To do otherwise could prevent the individual from achieving the greatest possible net benefit within the limits of the person's income. Similarly, no economically rational society would purchase a good — including pollution abatement — without considering both its benefit and its cost. As with the individual, to do otherwise would jeopardize the ability of society to achieve the greatest possible net benefit within the limits of society's income. We have already analyzed the socially efficient levels of gasoline consumption and electricity production. Similar logic allows us to analyze the socially efficient level of pollution abatement. Two further steps are helpful in developing our analysis of the optimal level of pollution abatement, one relating to social benefit and the other to social cost.

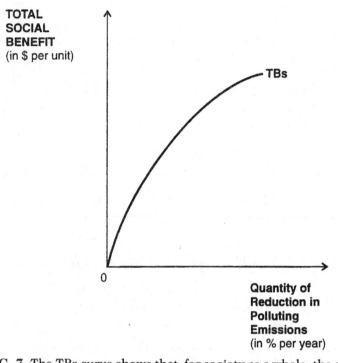

FIG. 7. The TBs curve shows that, for society as a whole, the sum of the private and public benefit from reductions in polluting emissions (measured on the vertical axis) rises at a decreasing rate as the amount of reduction in polluting emissions, in percent reduced per year (measured on the horizontal axis), increases.

The Social Benefit of Pollution Abatement

Total social benefit, shown as the TBs curve in Figure 7, refers *to the sum of all private and public benefit* that society derives from reductions in polluting emissions. The total social benefit of pollution abatement continuously increases, i.e., every increase in pollution abatement yields some additional social benefit. However, *each additional, reduction of, say, one percent in pollution yields less benefit to society than the preceding reduction of one percent in pollution.* This result means that the marginal social benefit of pollution abatement declines as society purchases more pollution abatement, as shown by the MBs curve in Figure 8[1]. The logic behind the declining marginal social benefit of pollution abatement is simple. When society purchases relatively little pollution abatement, air quality initially is quite poor. At this point, even small improvements in

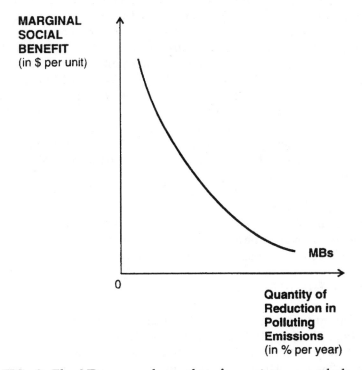

FIG. 8. The MBs curve shows that, for society as a whole, the marginal private plus public benefit from reductions in polluting emissions (measured on the vertical axis) continuously decreases as the amount of reduction in polluting emissions, in percent reduced per year (measured on the horizontal axis), increases.

air quality provide very large benefits. Improvements in air quality are easily noticeable, especially to those susceptible to the damaging effects of air pollution, and perhaps even literally save lives. Air quality improvements in this range, therefore, are more valuable than subsequent improvements, when already reasonably good air quality is made even better and the positive health effects are less dramatic.

The Social Cost of Pollution Abatement

A second analytical refinement is the introduction of a more realistic treatment of technology and cost. Pollution abatement is not generally achieved with constant marginal cost, such as shown in Figure 6. Rather, each successive unit of abatement typically costs more than the preceding unit of abatement. This fact creates, in Breyer's words, the problem of

"the last 10 percent" or "going the last mile."[2] One former EPA administrator expressed the problem in terms of Superfund site cleanup requirements: "About 95 percent of the toxic material could be removed from
waste sites in a few months, but years are spent trying to remove the last
little bit."[3] Similarly, in an early study on water pollution by Kneese and
Schultz for the Brookings Institution, it was estimated that $61 billion (in
1970s prices) would be required to clean-up 85-90 percent of U.S. water
pollution, but cleaning up the last 10-15 percent of pollution would require nearly as much, an estimated $58 billion. In the case of air pollu-
tion, producers typically can use relatively crude and cheap technologies
to eliminate the largest pollution particles, but much more sophisticated
and expensive technologies are necessary to eliminate finer and finer pollution particles from the air. As a result, the marginal social cost curve of
achieving air pollution abatement, the MCs curve in Figure 9, increases as
the level of abatement increases; a steeper slope at higher levels of pollution abatement is shown because later units of pollution abatement are
much more expensive to achieve than earlier units of abatement.

The Optimal Level of Pollution Abatement

The upward-sloping MCs curve in Figure 9 is plotted together with
the downward-sloping marginal social benefit MBs curve previously developed in Figure 8. Society's optimal level of air pollution abatement is found
at point x in Figure 9, which in this example indicates a 60 percent reduction in air pollution to achieve optimal efficiency. The horizontal axis in
Figure 9, which measures quantity of reduction in pollutants, can also be
interpreted to read lower air quality moving toward the left-hand side and
higher air quality moving toward the right-hand side. Therefore, it is implied that point x also denotes society's optimal level of air quality. *The
socially optimal level of air pollution abatement does not mean achieving the cleanest air, nor does the optimal level of air quality mean the
highest air quality. The socially optimal level of pollution abatement is
the most efficient level of abatement as determined by: (a) How society
values environmental goals like clean air; (b) how individuals value the
private consumption of goods other than pollution abatement, like driving cars, which may directly conflict with environmental goals; and (c)
the cost structures of achieving both private and social goods, including
air pollution abatement.*

Changes in Pollution Abatement Benefits

The concept of the socially optimal level of pollution abatement is
quite general and adaptable. It can easily incorporate changes in society's
valuation of pollution abatement benefits as well as changes in external
and private abatement costs. For example, advances in medical science

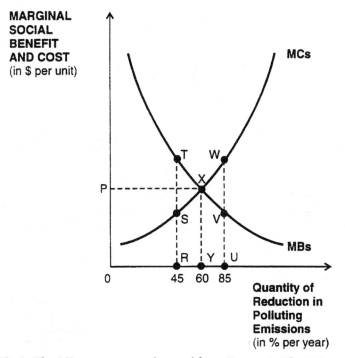

FIG. 9. The MBs curve is unchanged from Figure 8. The MCs curve shows that, for society as a whole, the marginal private and public cost of achieving reductions in polluting emissions (measured on the vertical axis) continuously rises as the amount of reduction in polluting emissions, in percent reduced per year (measured on the horizontal axis), increases.

are discovered and published almost every day that help clarify and refine our knowledge about the health effects of pollution. As one illustration, if medical science discovered that the nitrogen oxides in air pollution were less likely to lead to viral infections and lung irritation, then the marginal social benefit derived from NOx pollution abatement would decrease. Accordingly, the MBs curve in Figure 10 would shift downward to MBs", and as a result the socially optimal level of pollution abatement would decrease. Because the known social benefit from pollution abatement has diminished, society would want to purchase less of it. At the new price OP", society also pays less per unit of pollution abatement, reflecting the lower marginal cost of purchasing a smaller quantity of pollution abatement.

On the other hand, if it were discovered that, say, the sulfur oxides in air pollution were more likely to lead to heart and lung diseases and

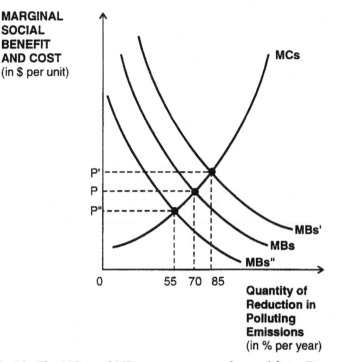

FIG. 10. The MCs and MBs curves are unchanged from Figure 9. However, compared to the MBs curve, the MBs' curve reflects a higher valuation of the marginal private and public benefit from reductions in polluting emissions; the MBs" curve reflects a lower valuation of the marginal private and public benefit from reductions in polluting emissions.

respiratory illnesses, then the marginal social benefit from SOx pollution abatement would increase. As a result, the MBs curve in Figure 10 would shift upward to MBs', and as a result the socially optimal level of pollution abatement would increase. Because the known social benefit from pollution abatement has risen, society would want to purchase more of it. At the new price OP', society also pays more per unit of pollution abatement, reflecting the increased marginal cost of purchasing a greater quantity of pollution abatement.

Changes in Pollution Abatement Cost

Even more intriguing than possible changes in the benefits of pollution abatement are possible changes in the cost of achieving pollution abatement. Developments in pollution abatement technologies are continuously occurring that improve and expand the technical means of reducing pollution. These new technologies often show ways of remediating and removing polluting agents from the air, water, and land more effectively and more cheaply. Two recent examples can be cited. One concerns the new technology of "soil-washing." At one Superfund site in Edison, New Jersey, the former location of a chemical insecticide factory, the EPA found evidence of arsenic, DDT, and a poison called dinoseb, all of which contaminate soil and create the danger of ground water contamination through seepage. The standard treatment of this type of pollution is either laying a permanent clay liner under the contaminated area and capping it with new topsoil (at a cost of $25 million at this particular Superfund site), or excavating and incinerating the contaminated soil (at a cost of between $70 million and $180 million). However, a new process of washing the tainted soil with a combination of water and alcohol could eliminate 91 percent of the soil contaminants at this site for a cost of only $7 million. Unfortunately, EPA officials rejected the new technology at the Edison site in favor of the older, more expensive technologies, even though incineration of the contaminants risks the release of hazardous materials into the air and a permanent clay liner with a topsoil cap leaves the area permanently contaminated.[4]

Another emerging new technology which could dramatically lower abatement costs relates to treating toxic materials at contaminated sites with enhanced micro-organisms. This is a bioremediation process and relies upon "biodiversity," which refers to the use of different strains of micro-organisms to attack toxic materials. After isolating particular micro-organisms by taking samples, researchers use forced evolution through gene cloning to develop the most effective strains of organisms for attacking the contaminants at a particular cleanup site. One of the largest and most successful bioremediation projects undertaken to date occurred at a former Sunoco fuel storage site at Toronto's industrial port. The cleanup process, which cost $1.4 million, involved encasing 85,000 tons of soil laden with gasoline, diesel, fuel oil, furnace fuel, and grease in a plastic "biocell" the size of a football field. Air, water, and fertilizer were then piped in to encourage the population of bacteria to multiply. "We dealt with the problem here," said one Sunoco manager, "rather then exporting it to a landfill."[5] The whole operation, which cost one-third as much as the dig-and-dump method, is an example of how technology offers new ways of managing pollution problems, both environmentally and economically. A recent Rutgers University report estimates that bioremediation technology could reduce the soil cleanup costs at typical Superfund sites by up to 65 percent.

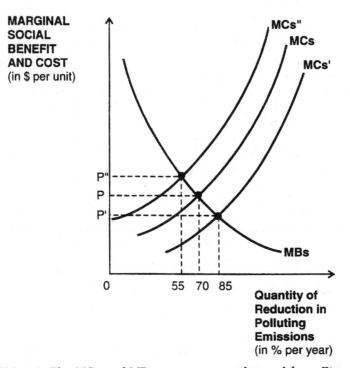

FIG. 11. The MCs and MBs curves are unchanged from Figure 9. However, compared to the MCs curve, the MCs' curve reflects a lower structure of the marginal private plus public cost of achieving reductions in polluting emissions; the MCs" curve reflects a higher structure of the marginal private plus public cost of achieving reductions in polluting emissions.

If new technologies like these were adopted, the MCs curve in Figure 11 would shift downward to MCs', and the socially optimal level of pollution abatement would increase. Because the per unit social cost of achieving pollution abatement decreases, society would want to purchase more of it. At price OP', society pays less per unit of pollution abatement — because of the decreased per unit cost — while enjoying the benefit of more abatement. When the EPA requires less-efficient cleanup methods due to obsolete technology and out-dated rules and standards, the opposite effect occurs: The MCs curve shifts upward to MCs", which actually reduces the level of pollution abatement society purchases compared with the level of abatement that society would purchase using more efficient cleanup technologies. It is yet another example of the Law of Unintended Consequences.

Social Efficiency and Command-and-Control Regulation

The preceding analysis of social efficiency in pollution abatement suggests several conclusions about the command-and-control approach to environmental regulation. Quite aside from the good intentions and conscientious efforts of thousands of honest, dedicated public bureaucrats administering our command-and-control regulations, the command-and-control approach contains several inherent, systemic defects embedded within it.

☐ Command-and-control pollution standards are rarely established at a level of zero pollution because such a rule would effectively close-down many plants, perhaps even entire industries, and prevent consumers from buying and using many common products in everyday use. But when pollution standards are established above a zero level, it means pollution is allowed up to the permitted level *at no cost to the polluter*. In other words, polluters can pollute for free, paying nothing at all for the external cost they impose on society, so long as they pollute within the established regulatory limits.

☐ A command-and-control regulatory approach generally treats all consumers and producers the same as regards compliance with a rule or standard, even though in reality tremendous differences exist among individual consumers and producers. As Carol Browner, head of President Clinton's EPA, said, "The idea that one solution works in every situation is something we've probably passed beyond, and we need to recognize that. We need to become more flexible." Unfortunately, a command-and-control approach is inherently unsuited to achieving such regulatory flexibility.

☐ Regulators often do not know, or care about, the cost of achieving mandated levels of pollution abatement. Certainly they cannot know the costs and efficiencies of all possible pollution abatement technologies for all producers. Nor can they predict the impact of a given pollution abatement standard on total production costs, product prices, or output and employment levels. Since command-and-control regulation typically specifies the method, device, or technology of compliance, the individual producer usually has no freedom of choice over how to meet a particular regulatory standard. Even when producers have the technical capability of using pollution control methods different from those specified by the regulatory agency to achieve the required pollution reduction at a lower cost, they usually are prohibited from doing so. Consequently, producers have no incentive to seek, invent, develop, or implement more efficient technologies to satisfy required pollution abatement goals. Moreover, command-and-control regulation often has the unwanted effect of preserving and protecting established special interest groups against innovative newcomers. For a case study on the problem of command-and-control inflexibility, see the accompanying information box: *The AMOCO-EPA Joint Study*.

□ Regulators often do not know, or care about, how individual members of society value environmental goals *compared to* their private consumption activities. But any economically rational analysis of the socially optimal level of pollution abatement must consider private consumption benefits as well as social benefits such as those that derive from environmental protection.

□ Under the command-and-control approach, regulatory authorities rarely, if ever, attempt to balance the social cost of a pollution abatement standard against its social benefit when establishing pollution standards. Obviously, less pollution is a worthwhile goal, but people also have many other important goals, both individually and collectively. For example, suppose EPA standards decree that the level of air quality must reach 85 in Figure 9, rather than the 60 level, which is socially optimal from an economic viewpoint. The marginal social benefit of achieving an 85 level of air quality is u-v, which is substantially less than the marginal social cost of achieving it, u-w. The total social waste of resources that results from mandating an air quality of 85 is the area x-w-v, which measures the amount that total social cost exceeds total social benefit in achieving the higher standard. Similarly, it also would be socially inefficient for society to regulate an air quality of only 45 because air quality improvement above 45 would bring an additional benefit to society (r-t) far in excess of its additional cost (r-s).

Social Efficiency and Market-Based Regulation

In the real world, vast and important differences exist among individual producers. Variations exist in the age of each firm's plant and equipment, the competency of its management, the structure of its labor and other input costs, and its geographical location, all of which greatly effect its production costs. The marginal private cost of achieving pollution abatement also varies, depending in part upon each producer's cost of its pollution abatement equipment.

We have seen that economic rationality requires that society pursue pollution abatement up to, but not beyond the point where the marginal social benefit from one more unit of abatement equals its marginal social cost. When society balances the marginal social benefit of achieving a unit of protection or abatement with its marginal social cost, the resulting level of protection or abatement is socially efficient. But, because of cost differences among individual producers, *achieving a socially efficient level of abatement is highly unlikely when common abatement standards are imposed on all producers*. A simple example shows why abatement stan-

A Case Study of Command-and-Control Regulation: The Amoco-EPA Joint Study[1]

A recent case study illustrates the inflexibility and inefficiency that often characterizes command-and-control environmental regulation in actual practice. It also shows, in the words of current EPA Director Carol Browner, the "adversarial relationship" that can exist between regulators and those being regulated which "ignores the real complexities of environmental and business problems." In this example from the real world, we see operating many of the factors discussed in the text that lead to excessive costlines under command-and-control regulation.

The story begins in 1989 with a chance meeting on an airplane of two old acquaintances, Debra Sparks, who then worked for Amoco Oil Company, and James Lounsbury at the EPA. They talked about the various difficulties each had experienced while working on environmental problems and how much pollution went uncontrolled despite both the EPA's efforts and producers' huge pollution-control expenditures. In a spirit of friendship and cooperation they wondered if a joint, in-depth EPA-industry study of current pollution control methods might prove useful. Executives at both Amoco and the EPA at first regarded the idea as a dangerous heresy, tantamount to collaborating with the enemy during wartime. But, after lengthy discussion and skillful persuasion, the two organizations eventually agreed to participate. Amoco volunteered its oil refinery at Yorktown, Virginia as the subject of the joint study. Meetings got underway very gingerly at Amoco's Washington, D.C., offices, with the first three or four sessions dominated by mutual defensiveness and suspicion. Relieved by very few pleasantries between the oil company and EPA participants, little progress was made. Gradually, however, some of the cultural and language barriers between the two organizations were lowered. For Amoco, for example, "risk" was an economics term referring to efficiency, opportunity, and outcomes, while for the EPA it was a four letter word indicating nothing except political and health dangers.

When the group finally settled into its task of studying regulatory problems at the Yorktown refinery site, the members of both organizations were amazed to realize that no one knew precisely how to actually measure air polluting emissions. Even though controlling air pollution was, and remains, one of the EPA's central missions, it rarely measures emissions from industrial plants. Instead, it enforces detailed rules and regulations that spell out exactly what pollution abatement devices and equipment a plant must install. As standard EPA operating procedure, regulators from each of the EPA's air, water, and solid waste pollution control divisions make on-site visits every so often with long checklists, sometimes checking the height of a smokestack or whether a filter is in place, on the assumption the required equipment will lower pollution. But whether and by how much enforcement of the rules and standards actually reduces pollution at a particular site is not normally at issue, much less whether they reduce pollution in the most efficient way. The focus is on compliance with regulations rather than actual pollution reduction. Because regulated companies are busy complying, they too evaluate their pollution reduction efforts by their ability to comply rather than actual pollution reduction. The EPA wants its rules and standards regarding equipment and devices enforced, so that is what the regulated company does, usually no more and no less. The EPA rules and regulations are frequently not based on the most current technology and data, and they seldom permit adjustments on a case-by-case basis.

In a rare departure from EPA normal procedures, the joint study team decided to actually measure pollution at the Yorktown site and evaluate the results of the EPA rules on pollution reduction. New ways of measuring the various pollutants emitted by the plant — fumes in air, fluids in water, and solid wastes on land — had to be developed. Only then could the study team evaluate the best ways of reducing pollutants. To Amoco management's surprise, the EPA officials in charge of each of the three types of pollutants seldom spoke to each other; division regulators at the EPA operated from separate offices, maintained separate regulatory staffs, and enforced separate sets of pollution regulations. For such bureaucratic reasons _ plus a good deal of open hostility toward the joint study shown by rank-and-file EPA field regulators, who "think they're the good guys going after the bad guys," in the words of J. Clarence Davies, head of the EPA policy office — the EPA administered its part of the joint study from its Washington, D.C., policy office.

To measure actual pollution levels at the Yorktown refinery, Amoco and EPA personnel together devised various testing methods, such as drilling wells to test water at locations all over the site and installing a sampling probe atop a 130-foot smokestack. The main pollutant at the Yorktown refinery had long been known to be benzene, a carcinogenic byproduct of oil refining. At the Yorktown site, benzene-tainted waste water ran into pipes that led to an open-air treatment facility. Laws passed in 1977 required treatment of benzene, but it was not until 1990 that the EPA had drafted specific rules to contain the chemical. The EPA's benzene rules for the petroleum industry were based on a 1959 study having nothing to do with the Yorktown facility. According to the 1990 rules, oil refineries were required to build expensive, enclosed canals and water treatment systems to capture airborne benzene emissions. Amoco began construction of a new benzene treatment system in 1990, at a projected cost of $41 million.

Meanwhile, the site tests being conducted by the joint study team began discovering several startlingly new and unsettling findings. As actually measured at the Yorktown site, benzene fumes and evaporation from the plant's contaminated water were 20 times less than the amount predicted by the EPA's 1959 study. Even more unexpectedly, a major new benzene problem was found at the refinery's loading docks, where the EPA had never looked and had no regulations or rules. At the docks, where fuel was pumped into waiting barges, the joint study found that fumes were carrying 1.6 million pounds of pollutants into the air every year, compared to about one-third of a million pounds eminating from the open-air waste water treatment facility. "Those were astonishing conclusions," said one environmental official who worked on the joint study, "that the waste water was not the problem and that the loading dock was. At the same time, loading docks weren't something regulators were even

looking at."

If those conclusions were astonishing, so was the EPA's reaction upon learning that its regulations were missing the real pollution target. Armed with the joint study data, in early 1992 Amoco requested an exemption from the requirement that it complete the high-tech $41 million sewer system; instead, it petitioned to substitute special two-nozzle hoses (for a cost of only $6 million) to correct the far more serious emissions problem at the loading docks. The EPA rejected Amoco's petition, even though the EPA's regulations were contradicted by its own joint study. There were no administrative procedures to waive the requirements, said the EPA's Davies: "You invest so much in terms of [bureaucratic] time, money and political chits in arriving at one of these regulatory decisions that to go back and change it is something nobody wants to do."

Because it received no relief from the EPA requirement to install the expensive but inefficient water-treatment system, Amoco has done nothing to prevent the pollution at the loading docks. "It's not required to be controlled, so it's not," remarked an Amoco manager. The 1.6 million pounds of benzene still rise each year from the Yorktown refinery docks. The command-and-control approach combined with bureaucratic inertia meant that a simple and inexpensive plan to prevent benzene pollution at the loading docks, which would have cost $3.75 per pound of benzene pollution reduction, was rejected. Instead, a complex and expensive water treatment facility was constructed, at a cost of $125 per pound of benzene reduction, and the plant's major pollution problem at the docks was ignored.

Notes

1. The basic facts about the Amoco-EPA joint study were reported by Caleb Solomon in "Cleaning the Air: What Really Pollutes?" *Wall Street Journal*, March 29, 1993, 1.

dards should not be applied uniformly to all producers when efficiency is an important consideration. Assume the regulatory agency has decided upon a 25 percent reduction in a particular pollutant, say, sulfur dioxide emitted into the air by power generating utilities. Due to producer cost differences, a 25 percent sulfur dioxide reduction costs one producer $1,000,000, while the same 25 percent reduction costs another producer $3,000,000. To minimize the total social cost of the sulfur dioxide reduction, the producer with the low pollution abatement cost should accomplish more than a 25 percent reduction while the producer with the high pollution abatement cost should accomplish less than a 25 percent reduction, perhaps even no reduction. Of course, such flexibility in abatement efforts would be subject to the requirement that the two producers together accomplish the mandated average of 25 percent reduction in pollution. (It should be noted in this example that the stipulated 25 percent reduction still may not be socially efficient because it was specified without reference to balancing social benefit against social cost.)

Allocating different pollution reduction efforts among different producers depending on differences in their costs can seem like an impossibly complex regulatory task, particularly since the regulatory authority likely has little or no knowledge about each producer's actual costs. Indeed, it is an impossibly complex regulatory task under command-and-control regulation. However, the task is not only technically feasible, but can be administratively simple and relatively inexpensive as well. Implementing a market-based regulatory approach and establishing a market in tradable emissions permits are the necessary steps in achieving an economically efficient regulation.

Tradable Emissions Permits

Although the dominant environmental regulatory approach in the U. S. is command-and-control, a government-sanctioned market in tradable emissions permits already exists, albeit in a very limited way. Its beginnings came in the 1960s, when the EPA approved an *emissions offset policy*. Ordinarily, the EPA would block new businesses seeking to start-up production in polluted areas (called "nonattainment areas," as opposed to "attainment areas" where the EPA standards are met) because of the detrimental impact on air quality. Without some measure of regulatory flexibility, however, industrial growth would be impossible in most older urban areas. Of course, banning economic growth in these areas would mean a resulting lack of new job opportunities where poverty often is highest and jobs creation most needed. Primarily to mitigate against the undesirable effect on jobs creation, the EPA designed an emissions offset policy that allowed new firms to begin production in nonattainment areas *provided* they arrange for a corresponding pollution reduction at another site in the area. For example, when General Motors wanted to build a new plant in Oklahoma City, the local Chamber of Commerce got local oil companies to reduce pollution from their existing operations to offset the anticipated pollution from the new GM plant. Similarly, the EPA permitted Volkswagen to build a new plant in New Stanton, Pennsylvania after the Pennsylvania state government promised to reduce pollutants from governmental operations to offset Volkswagen's new emissions.

One major problem with the emissions offset policy was the difficulty that firms often experienced in finding offset partners. From the producers' viewpoint, any system of ad hoc negotiations, which sometimes required direct governmental intervention, was far from ideal because of its unreliability. Instead, they preferred a more dependable system in which cash payments could be made as a means of arranging offsets. This is how the idea of brokering cash-for-emissions-rights first came into play. The idea led naturally to the concept of buying and selling tradable emissions permits.

The next step toward creating tradable emissions permits came in 1990 when Congress amended the Clean Air Act of 1970. Power generating plants and other sulfur dioxide emitters were required to reduce their sulfur dioxide emissions by half from their current levels by the year 2000. At the same time, however, the EPA began granting each sulfur dioxide emitter permission to emit a fixed number of tons of sulfur dioxide per year. Each EPA emissions permit allows the producer permission to dump one ton of sulfur dioxide into the air per year. According to EPA rules, after the sulfur dioxide emissions permits are assigned to each producer they can be freely transferred. The logic of this system means that when a power generating plant reduces its sulfur dioxide emissions — either by

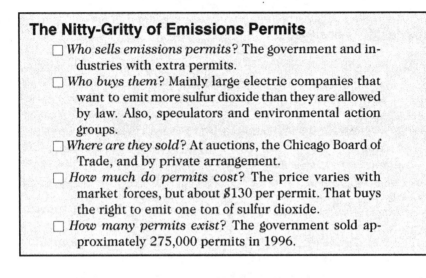

The Nitty-Gritty of Emissions Permits

☐ *Who sells emissions permits?* The government and industries with extra permits.

☐ *Who buys them?* Mainly large electric companies that want to emit more sulfur dioxide than they are allowed by law. Also, speculators and environmental action groups.

☐ *Where are they sold?* At auctions, the Chicago Board of Trade, and by private arrangement.

☐ *How much do permits cost?* The price varies with market forces, but about $130 per permit. That buys the right to emit one ton of sulfur dioxide.

☐ *How many permits exist?* The government sold approximately 275,000 permits in 1996.

altering its power generating technology or its pollution abatement technology — some of its emissions permits will no longer be needed. It is then free to sell its leftover rights to other producers who want to emit more sulfur dioxide than their allotted permits allow.

Since emissions rights could be bought and sold, this led to the final step of creating a functioning market to facilitate selling and buying. Thus, computer-assisted auctions of emissions permits and organized trading of permits (nick-named "smog futures") were born. Trading commenced at the Chicago Board of Trade on March 30, 1993. "Smog futures" trading and auctions expand the available opportunities for emissions permit sellers and buyers to make exactly the types of commitments they seek at market prices. Variations in the market price of permits equalize the quantity of permits demanded with the quantity supplied. Thus, emissions permits are now established as valuable commodities. Permit traders include not only the power generating companies, as one would expect, but also brokerage firms and private investors who speculate on future prices for emissions permits. Even environmental action groups buy emissions permits.[6]

Efficiency Gains from Tradable Emissions Permits

The efficiency gains that can be achieved from a system of tradable emissions permits are easy to demonstrate. Recall that negative externalities occur because of the failure of the market to price open-access common-property resources. Because of poorly defined property rights, these resources are improperly treated as if they were free resources, and consequently they are often overused by both consumers and producers. Resource overuse can be shown in Figure 12, where the horizontal axis measures the discharge of polluting emissions (for example, sulfur dioxide) in tons per year. The vertical axis measures the marginal private benefit from discharging polluting emissions and the price to emit these emissions.

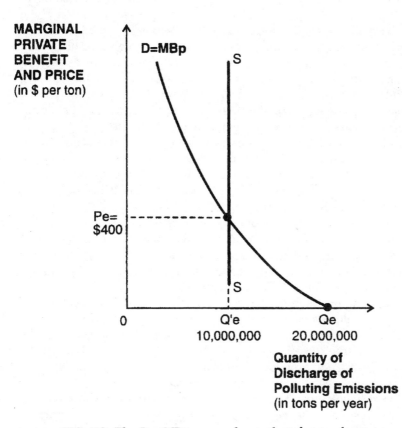

FIG. 12. The D = MBp curve shows that, for producers as a whole, the marginal private benefit of discharging polluting emissions — and the price producers would be willing to pay to discharge them (measured on the vertical axis) — continuously decreases as the amount of polluting emissions discharged per year by producers (measured on the horizontal axis) increases. The SS curve represents a fixed supply of emissions permits (corresponding to 10,000,000 tons of emissions) available to producers as a group.

Recall that a demand curve shows the maximum prices individuals and firms would pay for alternative quantities of a good or a resource based on the marginal private benefit from using the good or resource. The D=MBp curve in Figure 12 shows the maximum prices producers would pay to dump various quantities of polluting wastes based on their marginal private benefit from dumping polluting wastes. The D=MBp curve has a negative slope because producers receive a continuously decreasing marginal private benefit from discharging higher quantities of polluting emissions. The reason producers receive declining marginal private benefit from higher levels of pollution dumping is simple: the first units of pollution abatement (say, from 20,000,000 tons to 19,000,000 tons) are much easier and cheaper for producers to achieve than later units of pollution abatement (say, from 10,000,000 tons to 9,000,000 tons). In practice, firms can usually utilize relatively crude and cheap technologies to eliminate the largest pollution particles, but increasingly more sophisticated and expensive technologies are required to eliminate finer and finer polluting particles. It costs producers less per ton to reduce pollution in the range from, say, 20,000,000 tons to 19,000,000 tons than it costs per ton to reduce pollution in the range from 10,000,000 tons to 9,000,000 tons. The price producers would be willing to pay to avoid pollution abatement decreases as the cost per ton of achieving pollution abatement falls. Thus, the D=MBp curve in Figure 12 is downward sloping.

In the absence of regulatory restrictions or pollution charges, private consumers and producers will discharge wastes as long as the marginal private benefit from dumping is above zero (since the price to them for dumping is zero). This result is shown in Figure 12 at 20,000,000 tons of emissions, or distance OQe. The common property resource is overused as a dumping place not because consumers and producers are evil people, but because society offers them a "free" resource in the sense that they pay no price for it. A market-based solution to the problem of market failure *utilizes the universal motivation of self-interest*. Self-interest is brought to bear when producers and consumers are made to pay for their use of open-access common-property resources.

The most efficient way to make polluters pay for using common property resources is for the regulatory agency to issue a limited number of tradable emissions permits each year to current emitters, as it now does with the sulfur dioxide program. A market-based system would rely on the regulatory agency to identify and monitor all emitters, but not to regulate their behavior in detail. *The number of tradable emissions permits issued would be determined by the desired amount of pollution reduction.* Suppose the goal is to reduce sulfur dioxide emissions by half, as Congress legislated in the 1990 Clean Air Act. According to the numerical example in Figure 12, if one tradable emissions permit allows the dumping of one ton of sulfur dioxide, then the regulatory agency would issue 10,000,000 emissions permits to achieve a 50 percent reduction from the previous level of 20,000,000 tons of emissions. The supply of emissions permits available to all emitters is shown by the fixed supply curve SS in Figure 12. The intersection of the demand curve for dumping, D=MBp, with the available supply of emissions permits establishes a market price equal to $400 per ton of sulfur dioxide. At this price, emissions would immediately decline from 20,000,000 tons to 10,000,000 tons per year. Furthermore, this pollution reduction would be accomplished with remarkable efficiency.

As a practical matter, how are efficiency gains achieved through a system of tradable emissions permits? We have seen that individual producers differ greatly in their technologies and cost structures. Some producers have relatively inexpensive ways of correcting their emissions problems, including adopting new emissions abatement technologies and otherwise changing their production processes. These producers have a lower marginal private benefit from continuing to pollute than do other firms that have a higher cost of reducing their emissions. At a market price of $400 for a one-ton emissions permit, the producer who can eliminate one ton of sulfur dioxide emissions inexpensively, for, say, $200, has an economic incentive to do so; by reducing emissions one ton, it can sell an unneeded emissions permit at the market price of $400. The addition to the firm's cost is $200 (to reduce its emissions by one ton), the addition to its revenue is $400 (the proceeds from selling its one-ton emissions permit), and therefore firm profits are increased by $200.

On the other hand, producers whose marginal private cost of emissions abatement exceeds $400/ton would be the buyers in the emissions permit market. To understand the social gain here, suppose that the producer with higher abatement cost must spend $800 to eliminate a ton of sulfur dioxide wastes. If the regulatory authority ordered all producers to reduce their emissions by one ton without regard to their cost differentials, the combined cost of two tons of emissions abatement would be $1,000 ($200 for the first producer, $800 for the second one). With tradable emissions permits, the same two tons of emissions abatement is achievable for a total cost of $400 because the lower-cost producer accomplishes the entire two tons of abatement for $200/ton. It is in the self-interest of the higher-cost producer to pay the lower-cost producer through the sale and purchase of a one-ton emissions permit. As we have seen, the profit incentive for the lower-cost producer is a profit gain of $200; for the higher-cost producer the gain is $400 (the $800 cost of one-ton of emissions abatement the company has avoided, less $400 it pays for the one-ton emissions permit).

With the market approach, each producer is free to pursue its own most efficient emissions-reducing strategy and technology. In making their choices, the managements of each of the hundreds of thousands of individual firms possess information about their particular production processes and cost structures that no regulatory authority could ever possess. The regulatory agency administering the tradable emissions permit system would monitor the individual firms to ensure that no one emitted pollutants without the required number of pollution permits, still an important and difficult task. But this task is inherently less technical and administratively simpler — and thus more likely to be competently performed — than the tasks under the current command-and-control regulatory approach, which involve prescribing and enforcing detailed emissions standards and technical equipment specifications that are often beyond the competencies of the regulators.

A significant advantage of the tradable emissions permit approach is the economic incentive for all producers to improve their pollution abatement technologies and reduce their emissions. Both the producers who have already adopted effective pollution abatement technologies — and therefore who sell emissions permits — and the producers who have not yet done so — and therefore must buy emissions permits — have self-interested economic reasons for striving to reduce emissions. The market approach provides an economic incentive for continuous research, development, and innovation in pollution abatement technologies. Such an incentive is largely absent under command-and-control regulation in which pollution reduction standards and technical equipment requirements are usually specified by the regulatory authority. Environmental activists can also encourage producers to adopt new emissions abatement technologies simply by buying emissions permits in the market and holding them. By doing so, they would remove one ton of pollutant from the atmosphere for every permit retired. Purchases of emissions permits would not only reduce the available supply of permits but help drive up the permit price, thereby making it more expensive for producers to cling to their old technologies.

Actual prices in the market for trading permits to emit SO_2 illustrate how firms get smarter and more efficient in dealing with pollution abatement. At the time the 1990 law was passed establishing trading in sulfur dioxide emissions permits, the marginal private cost of SO_2 controls — and, therefore, the price of a one-ton emissions permit — was estimated at $300 to $600, with forecasts rising to $1,000 or more for future emissions permits. Actual permit prices, however, have declined to the range of only $170 to $250, with estimates rising only slightly higher for future permits. "In case after case," note two observers of the environmental regulatory process, Porter and van der Linde, "the differences between initial predictions and actual outcomes — especially after industry has had time to learn and innovate — are striking."[7]

Additional Steps Toward Regulatory Efficiency

The EPA also allows for a limited amount of flexibility and innovation in pollution abatement through emissions banking, bubbles, and netting.

Banking occurs when a producer reduces emissions below current mandated levels and is given an emissions credit, which it can either sell or hold for future use. Thus, producers have a bankable incentive to reduce their emissions below the current standards required by the EPA. A case in point occurred in 1992, when Mobil Oil Corporation purchased credits from a General Motors plant that had closed in southern California in 1985. The GM credits enabled Mobil to emit 900 pounds of polluting gas per day in the area.

A *bubble* is an imaginary dome placed over an individual factory. Emissions are then fixed within this dome. The producer may trade-off higher-than-mandated levels of one pollutant against lower-than-mandated levels of another pollutant so long as the total emissions within the bubble do not exceed the regulated limit. Bubbles enable an individual producer to use knowledge about its own production and emissions technologies and costs to manage its own pollution abatement activities most economically. This flexibility results in considerable cost savings for the producer while meeting EPA pollution standards.

Netting is an arrangement similar to bubbles, but with the difference that bubbles apply only to existing pollution sources while netting applies to new pollution sources. Thus, a producer can create a new pollution source if, within the same site, it simultaneously reduces emissions from another source. This flexibility would enable a producer, say, to cease manufacturing one product, reconfigure its factory space and capital equipment, and begin manufacturing a new product at the same site.

Bubbles and netting together have saved producers billions of dollars in abatement costs. Banking also has saved billions of dollars, but in addition it has generated valuable indirect benefits by helping producers locate new production operations in non-attainment areas where ordinarily the EPA would prohibit their entry. Needless to say, banking, bubbles, and netting all play a role in helping create jobs in areas where producers need a degree of flexibility in meeting environmental standards. The huge cost savings and other benefits achieved by these flexible emissions policies have not resulted in any overall reduction in environmental quality.

Notes

1. The marginal curve always reflects the slope of its corresponding total curve. Thus, the relationship between the total social benefit curve TBs in Figure 7 and the marginal social benefit curve MBs in Figure 8 is the same relationship we saw earlier between the total private benefit curve TBp in Figure 1 and the marginal private benefit curve MBp in Figure 2.

2. Stephen Breyer, *Breaking The Vicious Circle: Toward Effective Risk Regulation*, Cambridge, Mass., Harvard University Press, 1993, 11.

3. Breyer, 11.

4. Anthony A. Gallotto, "Pallone Sees Soil-Washing as Solution for Tainted Insecticide Plant Site," *Newark Star Ledger*, August 16, 1994, 20.

5. Mary Gooderham, "Bacteria Saves Time in Cleanup of Fuel Plant Site," *Albany Times Union*, December 1, 1996, F-1.

6. Jodi Ross Kahn, "We Won't Let Them Pollute, *React*, Sept. 18-24, 1995, 10.

7. M.E. Porter and C. van der Linde, "Toward A New Conception of the Environment - Competitiveness Relationship," *Journal of Economic Perspectives*, 9, 4, Fall, 1995, 108.

Chapter 8
Achieving Socially Efficient Pollution Abatement: A Simulated Task

This chapter presents an environmental protection task in an authentic context. The task gives the reader the opportunity to utilize many of the analytical concepts developed in previous chapters. The idea here is to understand the relevance of these analytical concepts and apply them within the framework of a simulated pollution abatement problem.

The Task

Part I

You have recently been hired by the local Air Quality Control Board (AQCB) in your region to explore alternative approaches for reducing the level of polluting nitrogen oxide (NOx) fumes that numerous power-generating plants and other large industrial boilers in your area are emitting into the atmosphere. The AQCB does not expect you to implement a plan, but it does want you to advise them about the best course of action in reaching a NOx emissions reduction goal through either the traditional command-and-control approach or newer market-based strategies.

Unfortunately, the AQCB staff lacks reliable data on either the social cost or the social benefit from achieving NOx emissions reductions in the region. Nevertheless, the AQCB has decided upon a regulatory objective of a 25 percent reduction — that is, to reduce the known current level of 1,000,000 tons/year of NOx emitted by the 50 largest plants in the region by 250,000 tons. The AQCB chairperson expects you to make recommendations on how the 25 percent NOx emissions reduction can be accomplished *most efficiently* in terms of *minimizing the total social cost to the community.*

The 50 targeted industrial and commercial firms in your region manufacture many different products using many different technologies. Neither you nor the AQCB staff has much information about the costs to different producers of reducing their NOx emissions. However, you do have access to one recent study for two firms out of the total of 50, Alpha Co. and Beta Corp. The study shows that these two firms have very different costs of reducing their NOx emissions, as shown in Table 8-1.

TABLE 8-1: NOx Emissions Abatement Costs for Two Producers

NOx Emissions Abatement Levels (tons per year)	Total Cost to Alpha Co.	Total Cost to Beta Corp.
1,000	$ 5,000	$ 10,000
2,000	$ 12,500	$ 25,000
3,000	$ 22,500	$ 45,000
4,000	$ 35,000	$ 70,000
5,000	$ 50,000	$100,000
6,000	$ 67,500	$135,000
7,000	$ 87,500	$175,000
8,000	$110,000	$220,000
9,000	$135,000	$270,000
10,000	$165,000	$330,000

There is neither time nor money for you or the AQCB staff to perform additional research to learn more about the other 48 producers' NOx emissions abatement costs. Nevertheless, you must offer advice on how to satisfy the AQCB chairperson's requirement that the total cost to the community of achieving the 25 percent NOx emissions reduction be kept to a minimum.

Since you have so little data on the different producers' emissions abatement costs, one member of the AQCB urges you to recommend spreading the required 250,000 ton NOx emissions abatement *equally among the 50 firms*, i.e., a 5,000-ton reduction for each firm. Another AQCB member urges the need to be "fair" to the smaller firms among the 50 emitters: He wants to impose NOx emissions reductions on each firm proportionate to each firm's contribution to the current total of 1,000,000 tons of NOx emissions.

You now must write a report that responds to the arguments of these two AQCB members. In your report, you must also recommend how to solve the problem of keeping the total cost to the community of the 250,000-ton NOx emissions reduction as low as possible, in keeping with the AQCB chairperson's wishes. You must do this even though you possess almost no information about actual emissions abatement costs for the firms in your region, except for the data given above in Table 8-1 pertaining to the emissions reduction costs of Alpha Co. and Beta Corp. Based on your knowledge of environmental economics, discuss the three possible approaches to your problem: imposing equal NOx emissions reductions for all 50 firms; imposing proportionately equal NOx emissions reductions for each of the 50 firms; or a market-based solution to achieve the necessary 250,000 ton NOx emissions reduction. In particular, examine the three approaches in terms of keeping the total emissions reduction cost as low as possible. Under a market-based emissions reduction plan, which firm — Alpha Co. or Beta Corp. — is more likely to be a buyer of emissions permits, and which firm is more likely to be a seller of emissions permits? Explain your answer by reference to the marginal costs of Alpha Co. and Beta Corp. in achieving their NOx emissions reductions.

Part II

After you have completed your assignment in Part I, assume a changed set of circumstances: Research data becomes available to the AQCB that provides some new information about both the marginal cost of achieving different levels of NOx reduction for the combined 50 major emitters in your region and the marginal benefit your region can expect to receive from achieving different levels of NOx reduction. The new data are shown in Table 8-2. (The data pertain to the situation in the region *before* the AQCB has had a chance to implement the required 250,000 tons/year NOx reduction discussed in Part I.)

TABLE 8-2. Marginal Social Cost and Benefit Estimates, for Various Levels of NOx Emissions Abatement

Amounts of NOx Emissions Abatement in Region	Marginal Social Cost of Achieving NOx Emissions Abatement	Marginal Social Benefit from Achieving NOx Emissions Abatement
1. from 1,000,000 tons to 750,000 tons	$1,500,000	$10,000,000
2. from 750,000 tons to 500,000 tons	$2,250,000	$ 5,000,000
3. from 500,000 tons to 250,000 tons	$3,500,000	$ 2,500,000
4. from 250,000 tons to 0 tons	$5,250,000	$ 500,000

Based on this data, you must now write a revised version of your original report. From the vantage point provided by the new data (and assuming it is generally reliable), evaluate the AQCB's earlier decision requiring the 50 major emitters in the region to reduce their NOx emissions by 25 percent (from 1,000,000 tons/year to 750,000 tons/year). Can you now be more precise about the socially optimal amount of NOx pollution abatement in your region? What would be your recommendation to the AQCB for achieving the socially optimal amount of NOx emissions abatement? Specifically, is the original mandate of a 250,000 ton NOx emissions reduction too large a reduction or not large enough? From an economic viewpoint, should the NOx emissions reduction goal be reduced or increased? And, as before, you must indicate how you could achieve any new NOx emissions reduction objective at lowest total cost. Again, discuss the three possible approaches specifically in terms of keeping the total emissions reduction cost as low as possible: imposing equal NOx emissions reductions, imposing proportionately equal NOx emissions reductions, or a market-based approach to any new NOx emissions reduction goal.

Your Response

Part I

The suggestions of the two AQCB members who urged imposing equal and proportionately equal NOx emissions reductions for all 50 firms are not useful in developing your recommendations because they bear no relationship to the firms' costs of emissions abatement. The little data you do possess clearly show that equal treatment of Alpha Co. and Beta Corp. would fail to minimize the total cost of any emissions reduction. If these two firms were required to reduce NOx emissions by 5,000 tons each, the total emissions reduction cost would be $50,000 plus $100,000 = $150,000. But if Alpha Co. were to reduce its emissions by 7,000 tons and Beta Corp. by 3,000 tons, the total emissions reduction cost would be $87,500 plus $45,000 = $132,500, for a saving of $17,500. The simplistic formulas of the two AQCB members may be emotionally and politically attractive recommendations, but they do not offer economically rational solutions.

Unlike most regulatory agency bureaucrats, the chairperson of the AQCB has an understanding of basic economic principles. She realizes that the producers in your region do not exist in isolation from the rest of the world, but are relatively small players in a national, or even an international, marketplace for the goods they produce and sell. Reductions in NOx emissions, while desirable environmental objectives, also mean higher production costs for these producers. They will attempt to pass along these costs to consumers in the form of higher prices, just as they attempt to pass along higher costs due to higher raw materials prices or higher labor costs. All other things being equal, higher costs of production put local producers at a competitive cost disadvantage vis-a-vis other U.S. and world producers. Indeed, the local producers may not be able to pass along price increases corresponding to their cost increases due to the NOx emissions reductions. In this case, the local producers may be caught in a cost-price squeeze, which could result in the firms reducing output or even completely shutting-down, with devastating employment losses for the region. Even if the local producers can pass along price increases corresponding to their cost increases, the price increases will likely reduce their total sales volume — remember that an inverse relationship exists between a good's price and its quantity demanded; a decline in the firms' sales volume will reduce their level of production and cause a loss of jobs in the region. Because she understands these effects, the AQCB chairperson is sensitive to the need to keep cost increases due to NOx emissions abatement as low as possible, consistent with the 25 percent emissions abatement target.

A command-and-control allocation of emissions abatement quotas among the region's 50 major NOx emitters is similar to the rationing of goods: it substitutes the judgment of a government agency — which means the judgment of bureaucrats — for the judgment of the market. This substitution is a very risky proposition when an agency possesses excellent cost information and it is supremely foolish when the agency has almost no cost information. The beginning of the answer to your problem is for you *to not attempt what you cannot possibly accomplish*; instead, turn the problem over to the market, which can accomplish your solution. Although you do not know each producer's emissions abatement cost, the individual producers do know their own costs (or will soon find out).

Although it is a difficult lesson to learn for environmentalists accustomed to command-and-control regulation, the 50 individual producers can best decide how to reduce their NOx emissions most efficiently. The *mechanism* that allows their collective knowledge to achieve the least cost solution is the *market system*. Your recommendation is that the AQCB give each of the 50 producers tradable emissions permits equal to three-quarters of their current levels of NOx emissions. That is, with one emissions permit allowing one ton of NOx emissions, producers would receive three permits for every four tons of current emissions, for a total of 750,000 emissions permits issued. Assuming that the AQCB enforces the rule that no producer emits more NOx than the number of permits it possesses, the total NOx emissions in the region will immediately decline by 25 percent (from 1,000,000 tons to 750,000 tons). A perfectly inelastic supply curve of NOx emissions permits now exists in the market, similar to the SS curve shown in Figure 12.

The cost savings to the community are achieved only after an emissions permit market develops and emissions permits are actively traded. Until trading in emissions permits begins, your solution is no different from the simple rule that every firm reduces its emissions by 25 percent, and we already know the equal-treatment rule is not the least-cost solution. Fortunately, the AQCB need take no bureaucratic action for trading in emissions permits to begin, other than to make trading legal. In their own self-interest, the 50 producers will spontaneously begin trading permits as a means of maximizing their profits (or minimizing losses) in the context of the mandated 250,000 ton emissions reduction. Each producer will decide for itself if profits are maximized (or losses minimized) by reducing its NOx emissions 25 percent to exactly balance-out against its number of emissions permits; or, by reducing its NOx emissions more than 25 percent and selling its unused emissions permits; or, by reducing its NOx emissions by less than 25 percent (or none at all) and purchasing the additional emissions permits as necessary. Whether an individual producer will be a buyer or a seller in the NOx emissions permit market depends upon whether its emissions reduction cost per ton is greater than or less than the market price of a one-ton NOx permit. Of course, each producer's emissions abatement cost per ton may be quite different from the others, as suggested by the data in Table 8-1. The marginal benefit to each producer of avoiding the cost of emissions abatement establishes its demand for emissions permits. There is no need for the AQCB to know each producer's demand for emissions permits. It is sufficient that each producer knows its own demand for emissions permits, which is based on its own emissions abatement costs. Summing each individual producer's demand for emissions permits establishes the market demand for emissions permits. The market demand for permits together with the fixed supply of 750,000 permits establishes the market price for a one-ton emissions permit. The existence of a market price for emissions permits reflects the fact that the atmosphere is a *scarce resource* and now bears a positive price for its use, thereby overcoming the problem of market-failure.

Regardless of the emissions permit price that is established in the market, *the permit price will cause the 250,000 ton emissions reduction to be accomplished at the lowest possible total cost.* Through the market for tradable emissions permits, producers with high emissions abatement costs per ton, like Beta Corp., in effect pay producers with low emissions abatement costs per ton, like Alpha Co., to accomplish most (or perhaps all) of the total required emissions reduction. In this way, the total amount of emissions reduction can be accomplished most efficiently. The equilibrium market price for an emissions permit will remain unchanged as long as the AQCB does not change the market supply of emissions permits and the market demand for permits does not change. However, the market demand for emissions permits will gradually decline as firms learn and discover new, lower-cost technologies for emissions abatement. Also, the market demand for emissions permits could increase as environmental activist groups purchase emissions permits and hold them off the market. Every one-ton emissions permit held off the market raises the permit price and reduces the amount of NOx in the air by one ton. The higher permit price serves as an incentive for every firm, whether currently a permit buyer or a permit seller, to discover newer, cheaper ways of reducing NOx emissions.

Part II

The economically optimal level of emissions abatement for the community is determined by equalizing the marginal social cost of achieving more emissions abatement and the marginal social benefit the community receives from more emissions abatement. This equality may require adjusting either upward or downward the amount of emissions abatement to the point where the marginal social cost of achieving the emissions abatement equals the marginal social benefit from achieving it. The optimal amount of emissions abatement exists at the point where MCs = MBs, or the additional social gain in benefit from the last amount of emissions abatement is the same as the additional extra social cost of achieving it.

From Table 8-2, it is clear that the marginal social benefit from re-ducing NOx emissions in your region from 1,000,000 tons/year to 750,000 tons/year easily exceeds the marginal social cost of doing so ($10,000,000 extra gain vs. $1,500,000 extra cost). As a matter of fact, the AQCB was far too timid in its NOx emissions reduction program. Table 8-2 clearly shows that *another* 25 percent reduction in NOx emissions (from 750,000 tons/year to 500,000 tons/year) is called for on *economic* grounds because the marginal social benefit from achieving it exceeds its marginal social cost ($5,000,000 extra gain vs. $2,250,000 extra cost). It is only at still higher levels of NOx emissions abatement that "the game is not worth the candle," i.e., when the marginal social cost of further reductions exceeds the marginal social benefit.

After you go on record as recommending to the AQCB a further 25 percent NOx emissions reduction, to 500,000 tons/year, you also recom-mend allowing the market to allocate the additional emissions reductions among the 50 emitters. Each of the 50 firms now should receive tradable one-ton emissions permits equal to *one-half* of their original NOx emis-sions level. The perfectly inelastic supply curve of NOx emissions permits that previously existed at a level of 750,000 tons (in Part I) now shifts leftward to 500,000 tons. As a result, the market price for a one-ton emissions permit rises, since the supply of permits has decreased. The market searches for the new equilibrium price at which the marginal private benefit of buying a permit (and avoiding one ton of pollution abatement) equals the marginal private cost of buying a permit. As the price of a permit rises, some producers who formerly were buying permits will now find it more economical to install emissions control devices rather than pay the higher permit price. In effect, the rising market price for permits has rationed these producers out of the permit market. Also, as the permit price rises, producers who were previously selling permits have a stronger economic incentive to reduce their emissions even more, thereby having more permits to sell in the market to take advantage of the new, higher permit price.

Chapter 9
Strategies for
Environmental Protection

Economics, Markets, and Market Failure

Economics, as we have seen, is the study of providing for the material well-being of individuals and society. Most of the economic tasks involved in providing for our material well-being are performed through an extensive and, under most circumstances, highly efficient market system based on voluntary exchange. In a market economy, private producers exist to create goods for sale and they earn profits when they accomplish this task efficiently. The pathway to profits is through satisfying the consumer. A market economy is fundamentally a consumer-driven system in which consumer preferences and willingness-to-pay are the primary forces that ultimately determine the allocation of society's productive resources. A competitive market economy organized around consumer preferences and willingness-to-pay usually responds quickly and efficiently to individual or collective needs and wants. However, when negative externalities exist, the general rule may fail due to the market's distortion. Negative externalities arise whenever the private act of consuming or producing a good inflicts an involuntary cost on other people. Negative externalities, in other words, are harmful side-effects of private consumption and pro-

Values and the Humanistic Critique

Economics largely relies on positive analysis because it seeks to understand how our economic system actually works and how the system can be made to work better in light of the constraints under which it operates. Economics also tends toward positive analysis because it strives toward scientific objectivity. Another way of saying the same thing is that economists seek to be value neutral. In most ways, economics succeeds remarkably well in excluding the individual economist's personal value judgments. In another sense, however the value neutrality of economics only pushes the ultimate values question backward to the origin of the values which economics takes as "given." The values that mainstream neoclassical economics assume as "given" are *the consumer preferences and willingness-to-pay that rational individuals express through both the marketplace and the ballot box as they seek to satisfy their wants and needs*. Our market economy is, at bottom, a consumer-driven system in which consumer preferences and willingness-to-pay are the primary forces determining the allocation of society's scarce productive resources.

On the other hand, most humanists — or "literary intellectuals" in C.P. Snow's terminology — adhere to a long-standing, highly respected tradition quite different from the perspective of mainstream economics and the priority it gives to consumer preferences and self-interested rationality. Both Platonists and Christian philosophers believe higher values exist that can be apprehended (correctly or incorrectly) and, once apprehended, must be respected. Failure to respect them would be immoral. If someone adopted a view, say, that extolled the innate value of preserving an endangered species or conserving certain natural resources, such a person probably would not believe that the neoclassical economics perspective of negative externalities and imperfectly functioning markets was relevant. To the contrary, this person might likely make the normative argument that consumer preferences and willingness-to-pay should not apply to ecological issues. While recognizing that humans have an impact on the natural world, the normative thinker would vehemently deny that a society can properly decide what levels and types of environmental impact are best by referring to self-interested rationality and tallying-up consumers' willingness-to-pay. Thus: "Human beings value a lot more than their own well-being," Sagoff wrote in a well-known humanist critique of economics. "Religious, political, moral, ideological, and cultural values are central to human experience and to environmental policy. These are deeply *human* values; they are anthropogenic in every way. Unlike subjective consumer preferences and like economic theories, these values reflect objective conceptions of the moral and public good."[1] Of course, to economists Sagoff has it backwards: Consumer preferences revealed in the marketplace are objective, not subjective; and religious, political, moral, ideological, and cultural values are subjective, not objective, at least until they are expressed either in the marketplace or in the polling place and backed-up by a willingness-to-pay for the consequences of acting on those values.

Notes

1. Mark Sagoff, "Four Dogmas of Environmental Economics," *Values and Preferences in Environmental Economics*, 3, 1994, 303.

duction activities that market prices do not reflect. When negative externalities exist, private consumers may not allocate their expenditure dollars and private producers may not operate their plants and factories in ways that maximize *social* welfare, although they will always consume and produce in ways that maximize their *private* welfare. Economists call such a result "market failure." For the economist, the preferred response to a situation caused by negative externalities is to remedy the market failure through appropriate market-based regulatory policies, rather than to abandon an otherwise efficient market system for highly inefficient command-and-control regulation.

Market-based Environmental Protection

There is no single environmental protection approach that is perfect, that will eliminate all problems associated with environmental regulation. The question is, which regulatory approach is most likely to succeed in most cases at lowest cost, and that approach is clearly a market-based system. In a market-based system, the government uses a combination of economic incentives (like payments or subsidies), penalties (like taxes), and tradable emissions permits, or allowances, to achieve its regulatory objectives. Tradable emissions permits reduce cost by having firms comply with performance standards rather than by subjecting them to strict emissions controls requiring the use of specific technologies. A tradable emissions strategy sets a limit on total emissions of a particular pollutant from all sources and a nominal emissions limit for each emitter. Individual firms can then vary their actual emissions through voluntary exchanges — purchases and sales — of emissions permits with other firms. Those firms that can curtail emissions at lower cost will more cheaply reduce emissions below their nominal limit and sell their unused allowances to firms with higher costs, who can then exceed their nominal emissions levels. Tradable emissions permits were implemented by the EPA in a national program that allows power plants to trade sulfur dioxide emissions under the 1990 Clean Air Act. Local and regional efforts along similar lines as the national program are developing as well. In 1994 Southern California implemented a regional emissions trading market for nitrogen oxides, which cause acid rain and contribute to haze and ground-level ozone pollution. Known as the Regional Clean Air Incentives Market, or RECLAIM, the Southern California program is broadly similar to the national market for sulfur dioxide emissions but with some variations, notably RECLAIM sets limits on the location of emissions permits that are traded to help prevent "hot spots" of pollution. A computer-assisted pollution-rights auction now exists in Southern California that includes both RECLAIM pollution credits and credits under the EPA sulfur dioxide program. Other geographic areas — notably the Northeast — are in the process of developing their own nitrogen oxide trading programs.[1]

Tradable emissions permits for sulfur dioxide and nitrogen oxide are not the only programs designed to take advantage of the efficiencies of market-based strategies. A promising alternative to command-and-control regulation of ocean fishing is the use of "individually transferable quotas" (ITQs). In a manner similar to air pollution trading programs, ITQs operate by setting a limit on the total allowable harvest of fish stocks and creating tradable rights to a share of the harvest. With ITQs, the harvest is undertaken by the most efficient fishing boats and the revenues from the sale of the ITQs are used to provide temporary financial subsidies for less efficient operators, who are bribed to leave the industry in order to shrink the total number of boats. ITQs are currently being used by two East Coast regional fishery management councils, on a larger scale in an Alaskan fishery, and in other countries outside the U.S.[2] Another promising application of market-based strategies on a world-wide scale relates to greenhouse gas emissions. As shown in the accompanying information box: *An Economists' Petition*, an international emissions trading agreement is possible, thereby achieving greenhouse gas emissions reductions at lowest possible cost.

Command-and-control Regulations and Its Costs

The command-and-control approach to regulation has a certain superficial appeal: If society does not want power generating plants or private automobiles emitting sulfur dioxides or nitrogen oxides, it has only to write a law or regulation or standard prohibiting these pollutants. Period, end of story. Unfortunately, it never is — nor can it ever be — the end of the story because the realities of a modern economy are vastly more complex than the superficial view suggested by simplistic thinking. Such mandates typically offer the least efficient means of achieving our environmental goals, whatever those goals are and whatever the desired level of environmental protection. Because of its inefficiencies, our present system of environmental protection has been accurately described not only as "litigious and counterproductive" but also "extraordinarily crude [and] costly."[3] It is, in fact, a near-perfect example of the Law of Unintended Consequences.

The high costs of an inefficient system of environmental regulation provide aid and solace to no one. The idea that "polluters pay" for environmental protection is a comforting thought for many environmentalists, and certainly the idea meshes well with a command-and-control approach to regulation. But, in reality, the idea is a non-serious intellectual exercise whose very serious effect is to detract attention away from extraordinary, often avoidable, costs of our current regulatory approach. It is inescapable that the American people, not producers, pay for most, if not all, of the present regulatory waste and inefficiency in what amounts to a very large hidden tax on the public. To believe that producers absorb these costs amounts to wishful thinking that environmental protection somehow is a "free good" to ordinary Americans. In most instances, producers are capable of passing along most, or all, of their regulatory costs and damage awards to consumers in the form of higher prices or to insurance companies, who, in turn, raise premiums to their customers. In those cases when regulatory costs cannot be passed along to consumers, producers can, and often do, reduce production levels or even go out of business altogether, resulting in job losses and a reduced selection of products available on the market. Since most environmental regulatory costs are hidden costs, the full costs of our environmental protection efforts are rarely, if ever, known and properly evaluated. It is equally true that many costs of *not* properly regulating the environment also are hidden costs, which take the form of pollution damage and environmental degradation. This result is common due to the lack of effective "Green Accounting."

Aside from its high costs, perhaps the most significant long-term damage generated by our command-and-control approach to environmental regulation has been the creation of an adversarial approach to environmental protection that poisons relationships among government bureau-

An Economists' Petition

In early 1997 a petition dealing with an important environmental concern was prepared by a group of five world famous economists, including several past winners of the Nobel Prize in economics. The petition was mailed to thousands of economists who were members of the American Economic Association for their endorsement.

The petition's cover-letter stated, in part: "As you may know, representatives of the world's nations will convene in Kyoto in December, 1997 to negotiate an international agreement addressing the threat of global climate change due to greenhouse gas emissions. This presents a significant opportunity for the United States to exercise a leadership role in ensuring our long-term well-being. Conversely, a failure on the part of the U.S. government to put forward a well-reasoned position would be a major environmental, economic, and diplomatic setback.

As the climate debate unfolds, it is imperative that public policy be guided by sound economics rather than misleading claims put forward by special interest groups. For this reason, we invite you to join us in endorsing the attached non-partisan consensus statement on the economics of climate change."

The complete petition read as follows:

Economists' Statement on Climate Change

We the undersigned agree that:

I. The review conducted by a distinguished international panel of scientists under the auspices of the Intergovernmental Panel on Climate Change has determined that "the balance of evidence suggests a discernible human influence on global climate." As economists, we believe that global climate change carries with it significant environmental, economic, social, and geopolitical risks, and that preventive steps are justified.

II. Economic studies have found that there are many potential policies to reduce greenhouse gas emissions for which the total benefits outweigh the total costs. For the United States in particular, sound economic analysis shows that there are policy options that would slow climate change without harming American living standards, and these measures may in fact improve U.S. productivity in the longer run.

III. The most efficient approach to slowing climate change is through market-based policies. In order for the world to achieve its climatic objectives at minimum cost, a cooperative approach among nations is required — such as an international emissions trading agreement. The United States and other nations can most efficiently implement their climate policies through market mechanisms, such as carbon taxes or the auction of emissions permits. The revenues generated from such policies can effectively be used to reduce the deficit or to lower existing taxes.

crats, environmentalists, businesses, and consumers. When these groups view each other as enemies rather than as partners, effective and efficient cooperative efforts to achieve environmental protection goals become very difficult, if not impossible. "Environmental activists look at a Department of Environmental Protection permit," said one former state Environmental Commissioner, "as a license to pollute instead of as an application that has been approved by the DEP so that an industrial plant can operate within the law. By their convoluted thinking, every permitted applicant becomes a polluter."[4] Many other observers have commented on the existence of a widespread anti-business, anti-growth attitude that can damage not only overall economic efficiency and jobs creation but also the environment itself, which often has been held hostage to endless litigation.

Politics and Market-Based Regulation

Just as higher environmental protection costs to producers often raise prices to ordinary consumers and reduce jobs, lower environmental protection costs can lower prices to consumers and expand jobs. It is unmistakable that market-based reforms in many areas of environmental regulation offer the promise of substantial regulatory cost savings. These cost savings occur because market-based reforms adhere to several elementary regulatory principles that are basic to achieving cost reductions. *One*, market-based reforms create the maximum opportunity for innovation by leaving the task of innovation to industry and not the agency in charge of setting pollution standards. Opportunity for innovation must be broadly interpreted to also include allowing the producers in the regulated industry the ability to assign the necessary pollution reductions among themselves. *Two*, market-based reforms stimulate a continuous process of technological progress, rather than locking in any particular technology or procedure for abating pollution. *Three*, market-based reforms leave as little room as possible for uncertainly and ambiguity in the regulatory process. When these same three regulatory principles for achieving efficiency are used to evaluate our command-and-control approach, it is clear that most current U.S. environmental regulations have often been crafted in ways that keep costs high and deter innovative solutions, even to the point of rendering them impossible.[5]

It is unfortunate that so many environmentalists reject simple yet cost-effective market-based approaches to pollution abatement. Some environmentalists simply react against the concept of a market for pollution permits on ideological grounds. ("We cannot give anyone the option of polluting for a fee," said Senator Edmund Muskie of Maine in the U.S. Congress in 1971.[6]) Perhaps a lack of knowledge about basic economic principles and the functioning of markets plays a major role in such thinking. One thing is certain: The logic of how the market mechanism can achieve efficient pollution reduction is very little understood outside the ranks of economists. A survey of over 60 environmentalists, congressional staffers, and lobbyists — all of whom were *directly involved in formulating our current environmental policy* — found that *none of them* understood the economic arguments: Not a single person interviewed could explain the logic of why tradable emissions permits are more efficient than command-and-control regulatory controls.[7] It is interesting that, in environmental regulation as well as most other regulatory areas, most non-economists have a strong aversion to dealing with market failure through changes in incentive structures and a strong preference for carefully specified, top-to-bottom command-and-control mandates and rules. "Such specification," notes Schultze, "is the natural function of lawyers." The legal profession, of course, continues to dominate the U. S. Congress, the state legislatures, and the various regulatory bureaucracies. When government makes the decision to intervene in private sector markets, political leaders and regulators typically rule out manipulating economic incentives to deter undesirable actions because they tend to see reliance on market responses as interjecting what are, for them, elements of uncertainty, randomness, and unfairness into the picture.[8] At the same time, they typically do not see their own regulatory actions through command-and-control interventions as interjecting an equal, or greater degree, of uncertainty, randomness, and unfairness. Market failures are often viewed by the public and the media, quite correctly, as requiring governmental corrective action. But it is equally necessary for the public and the media to appreciate the large areas of governmental failure and to demand a more effective, efficient governmental response to environmental problems.

Notes

1. *Economic Report of the President, Transmitted to the Congress February 1996*, Washington, D.C., United States Government Printing Office, 1996, 148-9.

2. *Economic Report of the President*, 151.

3. Bruce A. Ackerman and Richard B. Steward, "Reforming Environmental Law," *Stanford Law Review*, May 1985, p. 1333, cited in Alan S. Blinder, *Hard Heads, Soft Hearts: Tough-Minded Economics for a Just Society*, Reading, Mass., Addison-Wesley Publishing, 1987, 137.

4. Gordon Bishop, "DEP Urged to Reject 'Political' Agendas," *Newark Star Ledger*, September 28, 1994, 18.

5. M.E. Porter and C. van der Linde, "Toward A New Conception of the Environment - Competitiveness Relationship," *Journal of Economic Perspectives*, 9, 4, Fall, 1995, 108.

6. Cited in Blinder, 136.

7. *The Wall Street Journal*, April 7, 1986, 54, cited in Blinder, 137.

8. Charles L. Schultze, "The CEA: An Inside Voice for Mainstream Economics," *Journal of Economic Perspectives*, 10, Summer 1996, 27.

Chapter 10
For Further Reading

Introductory Texts on Economics

There are a dozen-and-a-half to two dozen general introductory economics textbooks on the market, in hardcover and paperback, that provide a systematic overview of the functioning of modern, market-based economies. The oldest and most prestigious of these is Paul A. Samuelson and William D. Nordhaus, *Economics*, 15th ed., (New York: McGraw-Hill, 1995). Other excellent, slightly less advanced, introductions are Edwin Mansfield and Nariman Behravesh, *Economics USA*, 4th ed. (New York: W.W. Norton, 1995) and William A. McEachern, *Economics*, 3rd ed. (Cincinnati, O.: South-Western Publishing, 1994).

The Development of Economic Ideas

Those interested in understanding the evolution of modern economic theory since the first great economist, Adam Smith, over 200 years ago are best advised to postpone reading the original works of the great masters themselves until after experiencing an introduction to their central ideas. Absolutely best for an initial exposure is Robert Heilbroner, *The Worldly Philosophers*, 6th ed. (New York: Simon and Schuster, 1986). Also see Heilbroner's *Teachings from the Worldly Philosophy* (New York: W.W.

Norton, 1996.) For the best examination of the social and political changes that were an integral part of the nineteenth century market revolution, see Karl Polanyi, *The Great Transformation* (New York: Farrar and Rinehart, 1944).

General Texts on Environmental Economics

The early treatises are now somewhat dated but still worth the effort. Among the best are Allen V. Kneese and Charles L. Schultz, *Pollution, Prices and Public Policy* (Washington, DC: The Brookings Institution, 1973); Kneese, *Economics and the Environment* (New York: Penguin, 1977); and William Baumol and Wallace Oates, *Economics, Environmental Policy and the Quality of Life* (Englewood Cliffs, NJ: Prentice-Hall, 1979).

More recent books specifically intended to serve as college texts include Tom Tietenberg, *Environmental and Natural Resource Economics*, 4th ed. (New York: Harper Collins, 1996); Barry C. Field, *Environmental Economics: An Introduction* (New York: McGraw-Hill, 1994); R. Kerry Turner, David Pearce and Ian Bateman, *Environmental Economics: An Elementary Introduction* (Baltimore: Johns Hopkins Press, 1993); John Gowdy and Sabine O'Hara, *Economic Theory for Environmentalists* (Delray Beach, Fl.: St. Lucie Press, 1995); and James R. Kahn, *The Economics Approach to Environmental and National Resources* (New York: Dryden Press, 1995).

Specialized Works in Environmental Economics

Those interested in understanding some of the special problems in analyzing economic benefits and costs can consult Richard O. Zerbe, Jr. and Dwight D. Dively, *Benefit-Cost Analysis: In Theory and Practice* (New York: Harper Collins, 1994).

For risk assessment and regulation, consult Stephen Breyer, *Breaking the Vicious Circle: Toward Effective Risk Regulation* (Cambridge, Mass.: Harvard University Press, 1993) and Adam M. Finkel, *Confronting Uncertainty in Risk Management: A Guide for Decision-Makers* (Washington, DC: Resources for the Future, 1990). Also see the somewhat dated Stephen Breyer, *Regulation and Its Reform* (Cambridge, Mass.: Harvard University Press, 1982).

For some interesting empirically based analytical techniques (including an input-output model) applied to the issue of sustainable world economic growth, see Faye Duchin and Glenn-Marie Lange, *The Future of the Environment: Ecological Economics and Technological Change* (New York: Oxford University Press, 1994).

Controlling Pollution in Transition Economies: Theories and

Methods, edited by Randall Bluffstone and Bruce Larson (Cheltenham U.K.: Edward Elgar Publishing, 1997), evaluates the recent experience of implementing pollution charges and fines and the use of pollution permits as regards controlling point-source air and water pollution in Central and Eastern Europe and Russia.